The National Coal Board's Backworth locomotive shed was located (NZ 305719) in Northumberland, a few miles to the north-east of Newcastle-upon-Tyne. The shed served a network of privately-owned lines in the area, serving collieries such as Eccles, Fenwick and Maude. The location was very popular with enthusiasts, gaining a reputation for the excellence of its locomotives, which were well maintained both mechanically and cosmetically. The brick-built shed is seen on 4 July 1973, with a backdrop formed by a winding wheel and a red livery (common in this area) coal wagon of nine-plank wooden construction. Simmering outside the shed is 'Austerity' 0-6-0 saddle tank No.6, fitted with 18in x 26in inside cylinders. Built by Bagnall's of Stafford (W/No.2749 of 1944) it began life as Ministry of Supply No.75161, but was sold in April 1946 for use at West Hallam opencast site. It moved to NCB Backworth in July 1961 and, after almost sixteen years service there, left in May 1977 for preservation. These days it can be seen at the Caledonian Railway at Brechin, Angus.

From Backworth locomotive shed, a one and a half mile branch line ran north-eastwards to Fenwick Colliery, near Earsdon (NZ 314730). The colliery was shunted by locomotives from Backworth. This is Fenwick Colliery on 4 July 1973 with the headgear, and its attendant brick-built winding engine house, in the background. Steel-built hopper wagons are plentiful in the sidings, plus three different sizes of red-livery wooden wagons. Performing the shunting duties is 0-6-0 saddle tank No.16 (Robert Stephenson & Hawthorns W/No.7944 of 1957) which had just worked in over the branch from Backworth. There seems to be a pause in operations, with the driver taking the opportunity to have a drag on his Woodbine. Providing variety from the commonplace 'Austerity' class, No.16 was fitted with 18in x 24in outside cylinders and 4ft diameter wheels. The picture was taken in the nick of time, for Fenwick Colliery closed on 31 August 1973. No.16 can now be seen in preservation at the Tanfield Railway.

The Westoe Colliery railway was amongst the UK's finest and has a long and fascinating history which can only be touched upon here. This spectacular overhead-wire electric railway (electrified in 1908) ran from Westoe Colliery (NZ 373668) at South Shields to staithes (NZ 359670) on the River Tyne. Loaded trains ran down a steep gradient leading away from the colliery, through a tunnel, and then negotiated dramatic riverside spirals before coal was loaded into waiting collier ships. Early electric motive power was 4-wheel and Bo-Bo locomotives of German manufacture, later augmented in the 1950s by a small fleet of Bo-Bos built jointly by English Electric and Baguley's. No.12 (English Electric W/No.1794 of 1951) passes the site of the former St. Hilda's Colliery with a loaded coal train on 13 June 1988. The railway closed in 1989.

Morrison Busty Colliery (NZ 176508) was half a mile to the south of Annfield Plain in County Durham. It was connected by a short branch line to the Consett to Chester–le-Street main line railway. The colliery's locomotives also worked Louisa Colliery, Stanley (by exercising running powers over the main line) until 31 December 1955. When Morrison Busty was visited on 4 July 1973 there were three steam locomotives on-site, of which No.4 (Hudswell Clarke W/No.1514 of 1923) was standing disused on a rusty siding together with several redundant wooden wagons. No.4 was an 0-4-0 saddle tank, fitted with 16in x 24in outside cylinders and 3ft 8in diameter wheels. Sadly it was scrapped only two months after this photograph was taken, while the colliery itself closed on 5 October 1973 and was subsequently demolished.

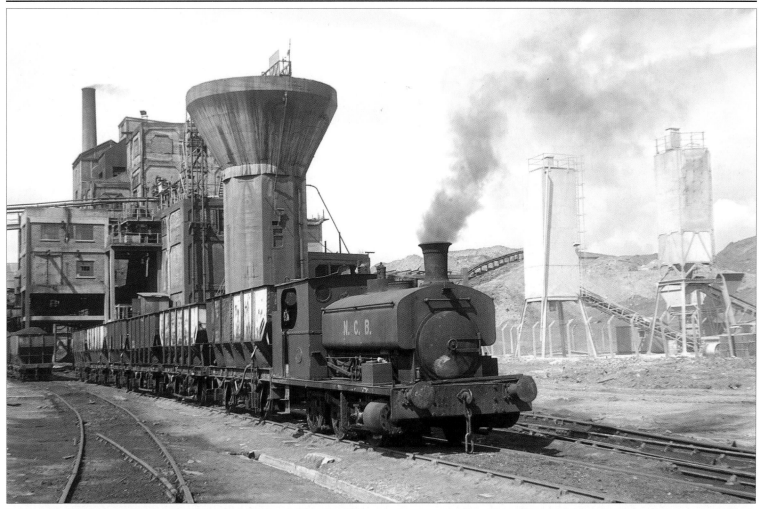

It was fairly common in the north-east of England for pit-villages to be named after the colliery which was the prime cause of their existence; thus Shotton Colliery (NZ 398413) in County Durham was located at Shotton Colliery! The colliery itself was connected by a three-quarters of a mile branch to the BR Stockton to Sunderland main line. In earlier days the colliery's locomotives also shunted Shotton brickworks and coking plant but, from May 1958, concentrated solely on the colliery. On 24 June 1971 a rake of six steel-built hopper wagons was being shunted by the somewhat work-worn Andrew Barclay W/No.1015 of 1904. This veteran 0-6-0 saddle tank was fitted with 15in x 22in outside cylinders and 3ft 5in diameter wheels. The colliery closed on 1 September 1972, but the Barclay was saved for preservation, and can now be seen at the Tanfield Railway.

The Tees & Hartlepool Port Authority was responsible for operating various premises around, and just north of, the River Tees. These ports, docks, and engineering workshops were all served by private internal railways. In the early 1970s the Authority operated a small fleet of conventional industrial diesel locomotives, augmented by three former British Railways shunters, D2023, D2024 and D2205. These ex-BR 0-6-0 diesel mechanical locomotives were all powered by a Gardner type 8L3 engine developing 204hp. On a sunny 25 June 1979, No.D2023 (built at Swindon Works in 1958) was shunting at Middlesbrough Docks (NZ 510207) where plenty of blue livery internal user rolling stock was on view. D2023 left Middlesbrough on 14 August 1983, bound for preservation on the Kent & East Sussex Railway.

On 29 January 1952 W/No.3715 emerged from the Jack Lane, Leeds, works of the Hunslet Engine Company. It was the third of a stock batch of four standard 16in x 22in inside cylinder locomotives with 3ft 9in diameter wheels. A short journey saw the loco delivered new to Primrose Hill Colliery, Woodlesford, Leeds. 3715 returned to Hunslet in December 1963 for the fitting (order number 59243) of an underfeed stoker system, before returning to Primrose Hill Colliery. On 4 March 1969 it was moved to the NCB's central workshops at Allerton Bywater (near Castleford) where, eventually, it was overhauled and repainted. The pristine locomotive, named PRIMROSE No.2, was photographed on 30 September 1971 after delivery to Peckfield Colliery, Micklefield (SE 438327); the Leeds to Selby main line is in the background. Fortunately 3715 was preserved and can now be seen at the Embsay Railway in North Yorkshire.

Wheldale Colliery (SE 441263) was at Castleford, on the north side of the Leeds to Monk Fryston main line. It was an excellent location with an overland branch to the neighbouring Fryston Colliery and, via running powers over BR metals, to spoil tipping sites on the far side of the Aire & Calder Navigation. Long after the colliery's internal railways had been dieselised, there was a steam working swansong in the autumn of 1981. Hunslet W/No.3168 of 1944 was refurbished and used, at the instigation of the Hunslet Engine Company, in certain tests on their patent underfeed stoker and gas producer system, as already fitted to W/No.3168. On a bitterly cold 9 December 1981 (when the photographer's hands, pen, and camera shutter all froze solid) the 'Austerity' proved its worth, going to the rescue of a 388hp Hunslet Engine Company 0-6-0 diesel hydraulic locomotive (W/No.7277 of 1972) which had succumbed to the frost. The 'Austerity' steamed on into 1982, its last working being in September of that year, before going for preservation at Embsay.

Bradford Corporation's Sewage Department operated both standard and narrow gauge railways at their Esholt Sewage Works (SE 185395) at the north end of the city. The standard gauge (which at its height in 1931 totalled no less than 22 miles of track and sidings) was connected to the Leeds to Keighley main line. The railways were used for moving sewage waste and detritus to tips, and also for transporting stores and equipment around the site. Over the years, sixteen standard gauge locomotives were used; thirteen were steam, of which ELIZABETH was one. It was an elegant 0-4-0 saddle tank built new for Esholt by Hudswell Clarke (W/No.1888 of 1958) at their famous Railway Foundry, Leeds. The locomotive (seen here at Esholt on 29 July 1972) was fitted with 14in x 22in outside cylinders and 3ft 3in diameter wheels. It is now preserved at the Leeds Industrial Museum.

Prince of Wales Colliery was situated (SE 451229) opposite the race course at the north end of Pontefract in West Yorkshire. The sinking of its first two shafts commenced about 1870 (by John Rhodes Ltd) and the colliery was in production by the mid-1870s. Its standard gauge internal railway was connected to the ex-LMSR Leeds to Knottingley line and, in total, utilised fourteen steam and two diesel locos over the years. The last steam locomotive on site was a standard 'Austerity' fitted with 18in x 26in inside cylinders and 4ft 3in diameter wheels. Built by Bagnall's of Stafford (W/No.2746 of 1944) it is shunting a couple of hopper wagons on 24 October 1975, having been called into action to deputise for a failed diesel. This interlude is believed to be the very last steam working at Prince of Wales, and the Bagnall was transferred to Ackton Hall Colliery, Featherstone, in January 1977.

The Hunslet Engine Company of Leeds was firmly amongst the established market leaders in designing and manufacturing diesel locomotives. They built early prototype, and later production batches, of diesel shunters for main line use, in addition to hundreds of locomotives of every conceivable gauge for industry. In the 1960s centre-cab diesel-hydraulic locomotives were very much in vogue for industrial use and, like many other companies, Hunslet produced such machines aplenty. Numbered amongst these was Hunslet W/No. 5590, which was ex-works on 25 March 1964. A stock loco sold to the NCB, it was an 0-6-0 diesel hydraulic of quite stylish appearance, fitted with a Gardner type 8L3B engine rated at 260hp at 1300rpm and final drive by side-rods and jackshaft. On a sunny 2 May 1971 W/No. 5590 (named HERBERT) was standing outside the shed at Markham Main Colliery, Armthorpe, Doncaster (SE 616046). Note the attractive stone building in the background with the gable end (left) showing MM 1920, commemorating the colliery's opening by Markham Main Colliery Co Ltd.

Rotherham Power Station (SK 421937) was by no means a glamorous site, but nevertheless had a very interesting railway history. It opened in 1901 and, in 1919, a connection was made to the GCR (later LNER/BR) Sheffield to Doncaster line; loaded coal wagons were pulled into the site by rope and capstans. The first locomotive (a 40hp machine built by John Fowler of Leeds) arrived in the summer of 1947, with a second Fowler (of 66hp) delivered in January of the following year. The station's third and final locomotive was manufactured (W/No.458952) by Ruston & Hornsby Ltd of Lincoln, and was delivered in 1960. In action on 22 March 1973, it was a member of the manufacturer's ubiquitous Class 88DS, a 4-wheel, chain-drive, diesel mechanical locomotive of 17 tons. It was fitted with a Ruston four-cylinder type 4VPHL engine and a four-speed gearbox. Rail traffic ceased in January 1976 and generation of electricity finished on 3 June 1977; the Ruston moved to Thos. W. Ward Ltd of Sheffield on 24 October 1978, and the power station itself was demolished in 1977/78.

Smithywood Coking Plant (SK 366953) was located at Chapeltown, a few miles to the north-west of Rotherham in South Yorkshire. The coking plant was operated by the NCB's Coal Products Division (later National Smokeless Fuels) with the NCB itself administering the adjacent Smithywood Colliery (SK 363953). Both Smithywood locations were served by a single track three mile BR branch which ran from Wincobank, on the north-east edge of Sheffield. The coking plant employed a single 0-4-0 wire-electric locomotive (Greenwood & Batley W/No.2543 of 1955) on the specialist coke car duties at the battery of coke ovens. Steam locomotives were employed for shunting conventional wagons which took away the coke. The wagons were mostly either coke hoppers or 16-ton mineral, although merry-go-round HEAs were not unknown. A rake of well-laden 16-tonners is being shunted by Hunslet W/No.3192 of 1944 (which sports a home-made chimney) on 29 June 1980.

Steam locomotives continued in use at Smithywood Coking Plant into 1982, making the site one of the very last in Yorkshire (and indeed the UK) with steam. Although a veteran 0-4-0 saddle tank (Hawthorn Leslie W/No.2454 of 1900) lingered on site into the early 1970s, the shunting duties were long shared by a pair of 'Austerity' 0-6-0STs. Their work involved positioning empty wagons for loading, and placing fulls into the exchange sidings to await collection by BR. On occasions they were also called upon to deputise on the coke car duty when the electric loco needed servicing or repairs. The two 'Austerities' were Hunslet W/Nos.3192 and 3193 of 1944, which were rebuilt in 1964 by their maker as, respectively, W/Nos.3888 and 3887. Following a snow storm on 10 January 1982, Hunslet W/No.3192 was shunting a rake of loaded merry-go-round wagons, with plenty of smoke and steam in the cold, clear, conditions adding to the atmosphere.

In the early 1970s many enthusiasts visited the Wirksworth, Derbyshire, site (SK 287548) of Derbyshire Stone Quarries Ltd (later Tarmac). The attraction was the little 0-4-0 saddle tank (built by Black Hawthorn & Company of Gateshead to W/No.266 of 1873) which was then reputed to be the oldest active industrial steam loco in the UK. Named HOLWELL No.3, this little gem was fitted with 12in x 19in outside cylinders and 3ft 2in diameter wheels. Tarmac Ltd was aware of its loco's celebrity and, on 28 May 1973, held an open day to celebrate its centenary, during which the Black Hawthorn performed various shunting manoeuvres. It is double-heading a rake of stone wagons together with the company's 0-4-0 diesel mechanical which was built (W/No.3357 of 1952) by E.E. Baguley Ltd of Burton-on-Trent. The Black Hawthorn can now be seen in preservation at the North of England Open Air Museum, Beamish.

Cadley Hill Colliery was at grid reference SK 279193 near Castle Gresley, some four miles to the south of Burton upon Trent. Originally sunk in 1860, the colliery's standard gauge sidings were worked by horses and ropes, later assisted by main line locomotives. A major reconstruction was undertaken by the NCB in 1961/62, involving the erection of a new coal preparation plant and the laying of new banks of sidings. At this time the NCB brought in its own locomotives for internal shunting. A very popular locomotive with the drivers was PROGRESS (Robert Stephenson & Hawthorns W/No.7298 of 1946); this 0-6-0 saddle tank with inside cylinders was originally ex-works on 13 May 1946, having been built to the order of the Moira Colliery Company Ltd. It is hard at work on 29 October 1980, shunting a rake of five loaded coal wagons beneath the Burton Road bridge. Rail traffic ceased at Cadley Hill Colliery in 1986, and the colliery itself closed in March 1988.

The Central Electricity Generating Board operated steam locomotives at many of its power stations, but the very last such establishment was Castle Donington (SK 433284) in Leicestershire. This power station was on the south side of, and connected to, the BR Burton upon Trent to Nottingham line. For internal shunting the CEGB maintained a pair of Andrew Barclay diesel locomotives (W/Nos.415 and 416 of 1957) but also two outside cylinder 0-4-0 saddle tanks built by Robert Stephenson & Hawthorns. The latter two were W/Nos.7817 and 7818 of 1954. The steam locomotives were used regularly in the 1970s and continued to work in the early 1980s. Here they are double-heading (on 19 April 1980) on the occasion of an AGM-day visit by the Industrial Railway Society. Thereafter the steamers were rarely used, but were retained on site – and this led to a notable event. On 30 March 1990, W/No.7817 was steamed as part of celebrations to mark the end of the CEGB before privatisation as Powergen. However, following a derailment, the RSH was called upon to deputise for a diesel and, by shunting a coal train, achieved the honour of working the very last revenue earning duty by an industrial steam locomotive anywhere in the UK.

Nechells Power Station (SP 098896) was adjacent to the Saltley and Aston areas of Birmingham, Warwickshire. Operated by the Central Electricity Generating Board, it was still an all-steam stronghold in the early 1970s. The fleet comprised two Peckett-built outside-cylinder 0-4-0 saddle tanks (W/Nos.1438 of 1916 and 1478 of 1917) plus three outside-cylinder 0-6-0 side tanks manufactured by Robert Stephenson & Hawthorns Ltd at their Newcastle-upon-Tyne works. The latter trio were W/Nos.7067 of 1942, 7537 of 1949 and 7684 of 1951; the newest of the trio is illustrated here. Hard at work shunting a rake of 16-ton mineral wagons on 17 October 1971, W/No.7684 looks somewhat incongruous as there is a gas holder in the background. The gas facility was operated by the West Midlands Gas Board and was also rail served – at the time of this photograph worked by a Ruston & Hornsby 4-wheel diesel mechanical locomotive.

Another Midlands power station was Hams Hall (SP 193920) near Coleshill, Warwickshire, on the north-east edge of the city of Birmingham. Opened in 1929, it was on the east side of the LMS Kingsbury & Water Orton line. Expansion saw the 'B' station opened in the 1930s, and 'C' commissioned in 1957. A continuous procession of wagons, including regular block trains from Griff Colliery, brought coal to fire the boilers. To shunt the wagons through the unloading tipplers fourteen locomotives were employed over the years (eleven steam and three diesels) of which thirteen were purchased brand new. In action on 22 April 1978 was No.9, an 0-6-0 side tank fitted with 18in x 24in outside cylinders and 3ft 8in diameter wheels. Built by Robert Stephenson & Hawthorns (W/No.7151 of 1944) it was withdrawn in February 1981 and can now be seen in preservation at the Bitton Steam Centre, Gloucestershire. The power station closed completely in 1992.

Construction of Hardingstone Road Power Station, Northampton (SP 763597) was begun during World War One, and the first electricity was generated in February 1919. Operated by the Northampton Electric Light & Power Company Ltd, the station was initially a small establishment, but quickly grew to four times as large. Ever increasing coal deliveries by rail meant that the NEL&PC purchased two brand new locomotives to replace a pair of old battery-electric locos which hitherto had done the shunting. The new arrivals were an 0-4-0 fireless with 17in x 16in outside cylinders (Hawthorn Leslie W/No.3829 of 1934) and a conventional 0-4-0 saddle tank. The latter (Bagnall W/No.2565 of 1936) was fitted with 13in x 18in outside cylinders and 3ft diameter wheels. The new pair were true stalwarts and thereafter worked constantly on the daily grind of shunting loaded coal wagons into the tipplers, and positioning empties for collection by the main line locomotive. The two were still together, and in excellent external condition, when this photograph of the Bagnall was taken on 23 March 1972. By this date the station was operated by the Central Electricity Generating Board.

Andrew Barclay, Sons & Co Ltd of the Caledonia Works, Kilmarnock, Ayrshire, was a prolific builder of standard gauge steam locomotives for industry. Its chunky locomotives were instantly recognisable, renowned for rugged reliability, and invariably very popular with their crews. This was certainly the case at Goldington Power Station, Bedford (TL 077500), where the Central Electricity Generating Board operated a trio of Barclay steamers. These outside cylindered 0-4-0 saddle tanks carried running numbers ED8, ED9 and ED10 and were, respectively, Andrew Barclay W/Nos.2353, 2352 and 2354, all built in 1954. When the station was visited on 23 March 1972, W/No.2352 was in steam, standing in the yard; it carried its worksplate on the rear sandbox, while running number ED9 was painted on the cabside and also carried on a cast plate mounted on the toolbox.

The use of steam locomotives in industry, which had been the norm for many decades, ground to a final halt in the 1970s and, in a few isolated cases, the early 1980s. It was indeed fortunate that, in this very era, the preservation movement was burgeoning. So it was that numerous steam locomotives, redundant at all manner of industrial works, were saved for posterity. A case in point was RING HAW, seen here in preservation at the North Norfolk Railway (TG 156430) on 23 May 1993. This loco, and its sister JACKS GREEN were originally ordered for use at the Nassington ironstone quarry, both being named after spinneys in the vicinity of the quarry. The latter (Hunslet W/No.1953) was despatched on 2 October 1939 and was thus the first Hunslet steam locomotive to be 'sent away' during World War Two. RING HAW (Hunslet W/No.1982) was despatched on 27 February 1940. Both were standard Hunslet locomotives, each fitted with 16in x 22in inside cylinders and 3ft 9in diameter wheels.

Brimsdown Power Station (TQ 368974) stood on Millmarsh Lane, Brimsdown, near Enfield, in London. It was notable that, into the early 1970s, its internal shunting was performed by a pair of 0-6-0 fireless locomotives. Built by Andrew Barclay of Kilmarnock, the pair (W/ Nos.1550 of 1917 and 1989 of 1930) were named SIR JAMES and LORD ASHFIELD. Fireless locomotives were characterised by having no chimney and their outside cylinders at the rear, beneath the cab, as witness LORD ASHFIELD which is standing on the left of this view of 24 March 1972.

When Fox, Walker & Co went bankrupt in December 1878 its Atlas Locomotive Works, St George, Bristol, was subsequently auctioned in February 1880. The works, goodwill, patterns and drawings were acquired by Thomas Peckett who went on to develop an admirable reputation for the production of small but sturdy industrial locomotives, almost entirely for the home market. Trading as Peckett & Sons Ltd, the firm found a principal market in South Wales, though locomotives were also sold throughout England. Peckett locos had classic, elegant lines, adorned with shining brasswork, each loco being of a class type designated by letters. Most locomotives were built to these standard classes and Croydon Power Station (TQ 305665) in London obtained a trio of R4 type 0-4-0 saddle tanks (Peckett W/Nos.2103-4-5 delivered in 1950/51) which were fitted with 12in x 20in outside cylinders, 3ft diameter wheels, and dropped cabs. W/Nos.2104 and 2105 are seen at Croydon 'B' station on 24 March 1972 although, by this date, both were a little workworn with brass somewhat tarnished!

Acton Lane Power Station (TQ 212826) was constructed in 1898/99 at Harlesden in London, and was but a stone's throw from the famous Willesden main line steam shed. Coal for firing the power station boilers was originally brought in by means of a wharf on the Grand Junction Canal, and permanently via a connection to the main (formerly LNW) railway line. Various extensions and upgradings were undertaken over the years. Throughout the station's railway history just six steam locomotives (and no diesels) were used for shunting. On 24 March 1972 LITTLE BARFORD (Andrew Barclay W/No.2069) was hard at work shunting a rake of 16-ton mineral wagons. Ex-works from its maker on 17 July 1939, it was an 0-4-0 saddle tank fitted with 14in x 22in outside cylinders, 3ft 5in diameter wheels, 5ft 6in wheelbase, Stephenson's valve gear and 720 gallon water tank, and weighed 27¾ tons in working order. It arrived at Acton Lane on 31 July 1965. By 1981 steam was a rare species in the capital and the CEGB held a special 'steaming day' on 28 February 1981 when its last two steam locos held centre stage, before both left for preservation.

Industrial engine sheds were every bit as fascinating as their main line brethren. They came in every conceivable shape and size, ranging from tiny ramshackle structures which *just* held one locomotive, running through two road sheds for four locos, up to ten road edifices which could house a fleet of thirty. They could be built of wood, brick, stone, or breeze blocks, with sides of corrugated iron, thick perspex, or rows of windows. Doors could be wooden or steel, hinged or sliding, roller-shutter or concertina. Roofs could be flat or hipped, with slates, tiles or corrugated iron atop. Facilities could be spartan, with perhaps just a wooden bench and a vice, through to a modern workshop with machinery and overhead crane. But whatever the structure, 'doing' an industrial shed produced just the same buzz as on BR. This is the shed at Snowdown Colliery, Kent (TR 246512) on 13 September 1979. In residence are ST. THOMAS, built (W/ No.1971) in 1927 by the Avonside Engine Company (left) and Hunslet Engine Company W/No.3825 of 1954 (right).

At one time it was the norm for brickworks in the UK to employ a narrow gauge railway, to bring the clay from a (sometimes increasingly) distant claypit. In general terms the procedure involved the clay being dug out of the pit by an excavator and loaded into wagons or v-skips. These were hauled back to the works where the skips were emptied. The clay was then passed through a puddle-mill mixer after which appropriate additives and colouring would be poured into the mixture. This would then be moulded into bricks, tiles and so on, which would be dried, and finally fired in the kiln. Meanwhile the narrow gauge skips were being hauled back and forth to the claypit, and so the procedure continued. Such activities were taking place on 11 September 1979 at Redland Bricks Ltd's Nutbourne Brickworks (SU 973375) at Hambledon, Surrey. Two diesel locomotives were working four-skip trains on a 2ft 0in gauge system between the claypit and the works. Motor Rail W/No.8678 of 1941 waits patiently as a Ruston Bucyrus type-33RB excavator loads the v-skips. The other loco (Motor Rail W/No.7199 of 1937) was dealing with fulls at the works and, in a few minutes, they would pass at a loop midway in the railway system.

Everybody knows that industrial railways have transported countless tons of clay, coal, ironstone, peat, steel, and the like. But what about watercress? The firm of Bedford & Jesty Ltd had beds in Dorset, for example at Bere Regis and Spetisbury. By 1986 the firm had changed its name to Sylvasprings Ltd. When their Doddings Farm, Bere Regis, site (SY 847947) was visited on 16 September 1992 two narrow gauge systems were in use. Hand-tramming (the word simply means pushing) of small flat wagons (loaded with boxes of freshly picked watercress) was in full swing on 12in gauge tracks on raised trackbeds laid amongst the beds. The boxes were then stacked on a lorry. A 'main line' of 1ft 6in gauge was also in daily operation, with a small locomotive (built in 1948 by Bedford & Jesty, but later fitted with a replacement 11hp Honda diesel engine) in regular use for moving men, equipment, and watercress around the lengthy site. The veteran is trundling across one of several bridges over the watercress beds.

Associated Portland Cement Manufacturers Ltd (later Blue Circle) had a works at Plymstock (SX 246542) immediately to the south-east of Plymouth in Devon. A deep railway cutting was gouged through solid rock to enable the works to be linked to exchange sidings alongside the BR line. To work the railway between works and exchange, APCM obtained a 4-wheel diesel-hydraulic shunting locomotive from Thomas Hill (Rotherham) Ltd, of Kilnhurst, South Yorkshire. Despatched from Hill's works on 26 August 1963, this locomotive (W/No.125v) weighed 28 tons, and was fitted with 3ft 2in diameter wheels and a Rolls-Royce type C6NFL engine rated at 178hp at 1,800rpm. In this era Hill's added one of two suffixes to its works numbers; c indicated a conversion, while v showed a brand-new Vanguard locomotive. When photographed on 18 September 1978, the brightly painted W/No.125v was preparing to run a rake of wagons down to the exchange sidings, with driver D. Veitch at the controls. Note the old car, registration number 303 UZ, standing alongside. The Vanguard loco gave many years of fine service, and these days can be viewed at the Plym Valley Railway, Plympton, Devon.

Falmouth in Cornwall has a maritime history amongst the oldest in Britain, its first quay being built in the 1660s. The Falmouth Docks Company was incorporated in 1859 with powers to construct a harbour, breakwaters, docks and warehouses – the complex (SW 822324) being provided with broad gauge sidings linked to the Cornwall Railway. The main line (by now GWR) and dock sidings were relaid to standard gauge in 1892, requiring that the FDC's three shunters be regauged. Thereafter the docks expanded, with their standard gauge railways always an integral part of the operation, moving stores, equipment, ship supplies, oil, etc, around the site. Just ten steam locomotives (and one diesel) were used over the years, the site becoming the second-last steam worked industrial railway in the UK when, on Friday 22 August 1986, No.3 undertook remunerative work. Rail traffic ceased about 1994. The notable No.3 locomotive (Hawthorn Leslie W/No.3597 of 1926) is seen on 20 September 1978, its elegant lines displaying 3ft diameter wheels on a 5ft 6in wheelbase, and 12in x 20in outside cylinders. It is preserved at the Plym Valley Railway, Plympton, Devon.

Kilmersdon Colliery (ST 688538) was at Radstock in Somerset. Sinking began on 6 February 1874 and the first coal was sold by April 1878. The colliery was linked by a branch (incorporating a self-acting incline) to the GWR Frome to Radstock line. Initially horses were used for internal shunting, the first known locomotive arriving in 1896. The colliery owners made a smart move when, on 10 September 1929, they took delivery of a brand new locomotive which was to give the mine over forty years of service. Built by Peckett & Sons of Bristol, the locomotive (W/No.1788) was of the maker's R3 class, having 3ft diameter wheels and 12in x 20in outside cylinders. The colliery itself was popular with enthusiasts because the self-acting incline was still in use into the 1970s. W/No.1788 is shunting at the incline head on 2 July 1971, with the winding engine house visible in the right background.

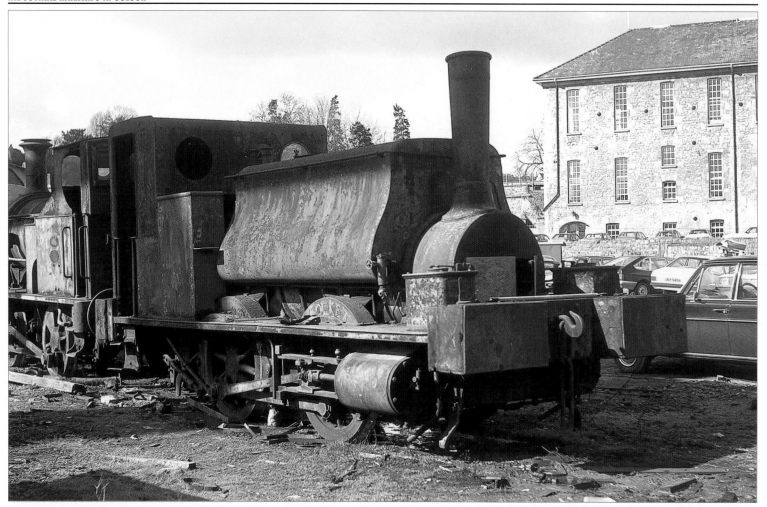

Another location which was popular with enthusiasts was Fairfield Mabey Ltd, a firm of engineers based (ST 538938) at Chepstow. Although its internal railway was latterly dieselised, the firm's popularity was due to a pair of ancient steam locomotives which remained on-site into the 1980s. The outside cylinder 0-4-0 saddle tank prominent in this view of 22 March 1982 was built well over a century before, in 1876 (W/No.2119) by Neilson & Company of the Springburn Works, Glasgow. Full of character, the rusting veteran sports inelegant block buffers, a tall chimney, and the name ROCKET scrawled onto its wheel splasher. Standing in the background is a little 0-4-0 well tank built (W/No.3063 of 1918) by Kerr Stuart & Co Ltd of Stoke on Trent, and fitted with 14½in x 20in outside cylinders and 3ft 4in diameter wheels. Neilson W/No.2119 can now be seen in preservation at the North Woolwich Old Station Museum, London.

The rather grandly named Aberthaw & Bristol Channel Portland Cement Company Ltd had two rail-served cement works in South Glamorgan. One was at Rhoose, and the second (ST 033675) at Aberthaw itself, both works being connected to the Bridgend to Cardiff main line. This view at Aberthaw (dated 12 June 1980) is typical of countless main line connections around the country which were protected by a small dedicated signal box. The box had pegged a class 37 diesel hauled freight on the main line, as John Fowler W/ No.4210114 of 1956 waited patiently on the private siding. Named IRIS, the Leeds-built Fowler was one of its maker's 421 class, an 0-4-0 diesel mechanical fitted with a 150hp engine, four-speed gearbox, and final drive by means of a jackshaft and side rods. At this date the A&BCPCC had five 421 class locos at its two works, all being named after flowers. The other four were BLUEBELL, DAFFODIL, HYACINTH and PRIMROSE.

The National Coal Board operated an engine shed and workshops at Mountain Ash, Mid Glamorgan (ST 051988). The shed provided engines for working Deep Duffryn Colliery and Aberaman Phurnacite Plant (to the north-west) and, latterly, Penrikyber Colliery (to the south-east). The internal railways were connected to the adjacent Aberdare to Pontypridd main line. The site utilised a small fleet of steam locomotives, including products of the Avonside, Barclay, Hudswell Clarke, North British, and Peckett companies. In addition there was an 'Austerity' 0-6-0 saddle tank (W/No.7139 of 1944) built by Robert Stephenson & Hawthorns Ltd. This loco worked for the War Department until it was sold to the Hunslet Engine Company of Leeds in November 1960; they rebuilt it (W/No.3880 of 1961) and sold it to NCB Mountain Ash. On 23 April 1979 it was pulling coal wagons from Penrikyber, and these days it is in preservation at the Pontypool & Blaenavon Railway.

There were many industrial railway systems around the UK which had privately-owned branch lines linking works and BR exchange sidings. Some of these systems became well known amongst the railway enthusiast fraternity, while others remained less so. Among the latter category was a scenic 2½ mile branch line in South Wales which was operated by Amalgamated Roadstone Corporation Ltd, and linked its Penderyn Quarry (SN 950088) to BR at Hirwaun. This railway was used by ARC for moving stone which had been sold to BR for ballast. It was shipped out along the BR branch line running down through Aberdare and Mountain Ash, while all ARC's other sales went out by road. On a glorious autumn day of 27 October 1982, the railway's sylvan setting is seen at its best as fourteen loaded 24-ton tare hoppers set out for Hirwaun. In control of the rake is ARC's 4-wheel diesel hydraulic No.2371, built by Rolls-Royce Ltd of Shrewsbury (W/No.10222 of 1965). This 34ton locomotive was fitted with a Rolls-Royce type C6SFL engine rated at 256hp. As the branch was steeply graded in places, the loco was equipped with supplementary air-brakes. Sadly the BR ballast contract was lost and the ARC railway closed not long after this picture was taken.

The use underground of narrow gauge railways was pretty much universal in British deep mines. For the transportation of coal, men, stores and materials, such conventional railways variously utilised hand-tramming, horses, rope haulage, and flameproof locomotives for the movement of rolling stock. In the late 1960s, however, a new railway principle was developed by Becorit (GB) Ltd of Ilkeston in Derbyshire. From 1968 they supplied certain NCB collieries with their new 'trapped rail' railways, an integrated system whereby unique locomotives and rolling stock ran on dedicated track. The locomotives were in three sections, with a power unit (driving flameproof hydraulic motors) positioned between two driving cabs. The track was of 200mm gauge and, simply put, was like a pair of facing capital letter E's without their central bars. High friction wheels gripped the top of the rails, with 'reaction wheels' hydraulically pressed up onto the undersides. The arrangement allowed fast and safe running without the risk of derailment. Becorit systems were normally installed in deep mines, but in 1971 Aberpergwm Colliery (SN 863059) at Glyn Neath opened a new drift where its Becorit system (with seven locomotives) could be inspected until closure of the mine in October 1985. Becorit W/No.DRL40/3/512 of 1973 was in charge of a manriding train on 24 April 1978.

The use of horses for underground haulage was once widespread in privately owned British deep coal mines. Indeed, prior to nationalisation of the coal industry on 1 January 1947, literally thousands of these beasts of burden would be in service at any one time, being stabled full-time underground. The NCB phased out their use, replacing them (mainly through the 1950s and 1960s) with flameproof locomotives. However, horses continued to be widely used at many drift mines in South Wales where they at least had the benefit of working out into the fresh air, and spending evenings and weekends at leisure in the fields. On 16 August 1994 horses CHARLIE (left) and LADDIE are seen with a few of their human workmates at March Hywel drift mine (SN 758030) in the hills near Rhos, between Neath and Pontardawe. By this date the Principality's drift mining industry was in sharp decline. By July 2002 only six known mines remained and the use of horses had finished.

Graig Merthyr Colliery (SN 624041) was up in the hills to the east of Pontardulais in South-West Wales. A single track NCB branch line linked the colliery to a stock site and engine shed (SN 599032) beside the A48 road at Pontardulais, the line continuing on to exchange sidings adjacent to the Llanelli to Port Talbot main line. The Graig Merthyr branch was well known for its 'paddy trains' which, because of the colliery's isolated location, transported miners to and from work. These workmen's services ceased in the late 1960s and, thereafter, the branch was used solely for coal traffic. The colliery closed in June 1978 and the stock site about July 1980. Latterly 'Austerity' 0-6-0 saddle tanks handled the traffic, and here we see Bagnall W/No.2758 of 1944 setting out from the colliery with seven loaded wagons bound for Pontardulais on 24 April 1978. Note the spoil tip on the horizon.

Most enthusiasts who visited Graig Merthyr Colliery also looked in at Brynlliw Colliery, Grovesend, which was located two miles south (SN 596013) of Pontardulais station. Brynlliw was an old colliery which was reconstructed and reopened about 1955 and, until its closure in September 1983, employed five steam locomotives. These comprised one Avonside and four Pecketts, which worked all traffic until an English Electric diesel put in an appearance shortly before the colliery closed. A minor road, off the B4296 Pontardulais to Gorseinon road, incorporated a bridge over the NCB tracks and provided a fine vantage point for observing steam operations. Viewed from this road bridge, Peckett W/No.2114 of 1951 is shunting on 9 June 1980, with the landsale yard forming the backdrop. A member of the maker's B3 class, the Peckett was an 0-6-0 saddle tank fitted with 14in x 22in outside cylinders and 3ft 7in diameter wheels.

Although Welsh coal mining is generally associated with the southern valleys, the industry was also represented in the northern counties of Denbighshire and Flintshire. There was a proliferation of pits around Wrexham and, at its height, the mining industry there once employed some 18,000 men. Bersham Colliery (SJ 315482) was sunk from 1868 at Rhostyllen, about two miles to the south-west of Wrexham and, when the last coal was wound on 18 December 1986, Bersham was the last coal mine in Denbighshire. Over the years ten steam and four diesel locomotives were employed on the pit's standard gauge internal lines. All the steamers were 0-4-0 saddle tanks with outside cylinders, of which the very last to arrive was Peckett W/No.1935 of 1937. This 14in x 22in machine (named HORNET) was transferred from Ifton Colliery in November 1968 and is seen shunting at Bersham on 23 May 1979.

Birkenhead lies at the north end of the Wirral peninsula, on the west bank of the River Mersey. An inlet known as Wallasey Pool was developed, beginning in 1824 with a shipbuilding yard, followed by a series of docks and quays opened between 1847 and 1909. Railways, linked to the main line, were laid all around the dock areas. The final major expansion came in March 1933 when Bidston Dock was opened. Rea Ltd, a company of master porters and stevedores, operated Duke Street Wharf from at least 1938; from about 1947 it became an iron ore import terminal. In the early 1950s Rea's took over operations at Bidston Dock (SJ 300910) which was also converted to a rail-served iron ore berth. Rea's had twelve standard gauge diesel locomotives; one of them, Drewry W/No.2724 of 1963 is at Bidston Dock on 21 May 1979, shunting hoppers (loaded with Brazilian iron ore) bound for Shotton Steelworks. The Drewry was an 0-4-0 weighing 32 tons, fitted with a 195hp engine and four-speed gearbox.

The highly successful 'Austerity' 0-6-0 saddle tank was designed by the Hunslet Engine Company of Leeds during World War Two. Fitted with 18in x 26in inside cylinders and 4ft 3in diameter wheels, the type was conceived for war use by the Ministry of Supply. No less than 377 were built between 1943-47 by Hunslet (120), Robert Stephenson & Hawthorns (90), Bagnall (52), Hudswell Clarke (50), Vulcan Foundry (50) and Andrew Barclay (15). In the same period two others were manufactured for colliery use. After the war, a further 106 were built between 1948 and 1964, by Hunslet (96), Yorkshire Engine Company (8) and Robert Stephenson & Hawthorns (2). These were for the NCB (77), steel industry (15) and the Army (14). Thus a grand total of 485 were made, some of which were re-sold for use on BR where they were designated Class J94. They were highly regarded wherever they were used and Bold Colliery (SJ 549935) at St Helens had three into the early 1980s – Hunslet W/No.3694 of 1950 was there on 1 October 1980.

The finest place to watch 'Austerity' 0-6-0STs in action was possibly Bickershaw Colliery, at Plank Lane, Leigh, to the west of Manchester. Located alongside the Leigh branch of the Leeds & Liverpool Canal (SJ 631999), this colliery was developed from 1872. It had a wonderful set of four headgears, but for onlookers the principal attraction was the spectacle of steam locomotives attacking the steep gradient from the colliery up to the exchange sidings at Abram. The pit latterly had an allocation of five 'Austerity' saddle tanks which worked, albeit only just, into the 1980s. On 14 April 1980 Hunslet W/Nos. 3776 of 1952 and 3823 of 1954 put on a spectacular display as they worked a rake of merry-go-round wagons up to Abram. On this date diesels had already arrived at Bickershaw and steam's days were numbered; the pit itself closed on 27 March 1992.

The Trafford Park Estate was developed on the south bank of the Manchester Ship Canal, to the west of Manchester city centre. Dozens of companies set up in business there, in part attracted by excellent transport facilities, which included the offer of a railway connection to a network of running lines laid all around the estate. These latter lines were worked by the MSC's railway department and were a hive of activity until the motor lorry gradually killed off the bulk of the estate's railway activities. By the 1970s there were but a handful of companies still utilising the estate railways and among these was cornflower manufacturer CPC (United Kingdom) Ltd. Its sole locomotive was an 0-4-0ST (Andrew Barclay W/No.1964 of 1929) which, each day, worked out of the factory gates (SJ 784979) and shunted sidings laid beside estate roads, as on 13 August 1972.

Agecroft Power Station (SD 802020) lay to the north-west of Manchester city centre, alongside the Manchester to Bolton main line. The original A power station of 1925 had a narrow gauge system but B and C stations (on an adjacent, but separate site) were provided with standard gauge lines to serve the new coal handling plant, commissioned in September 1950. To handle the traffic, two 0-4-0 saddle tanks were initially purchased from Robert Stephenson & Hawthorns Ltd (W/Nos.7416 and 7485). The fleet was supplemented by W/No.7681 (from the same builder) which arrived in September 1954 from Chadderton Power Station. All three locomotives weighed 28 tons and each was fitted with 14in x 22in outside cylinders, 3ft 6in diameter wheels on a 5ft 6in wheelbase, 700 gallon water tanks, and developed a tractive effort of 14,400lb at 85% working pressure. W/No.7681 was in the sidings on 12 September 1981, but is now preserved at the Steam Museum of the Great Western Railway, Swindon.

Industrial railways were once widely used for waste disposal at sewage works throughout the UK. These railways variously took the form of monorails, narrow gauge (hand and loco worked), and standard gauge, although these days such systems are practically extinct. Ashton sewage works (SJ 932973) was opened on 16 September 1903, at Dukinfield, just to the east of Manchester. It had a 2ft 0in gauge railway and, on 8 September 1978, the contents of a rake of side tipping V-skips were being emptied into a trailer. The yellow locomotive is Hudson W/No.LX1002 of 1968, a 4-wheel diesel hydraulic machine fitted with a two cylinder Petter engine. The loco was one of a pair of prototypes, both briefly used at the CEGB's Woodhead Tunnel contract, before returning to Hudson's – from where it went to Dukinfield in July 1971. It is now preserved at the Moseley Railway Trust, Whaley Bridge.

Heap Bridge is just to the east of Bury in Lancashire, and paper making there can be traced back to 1810. Yates Duxbury founded his Heap Bridge paper works (SD 828107) in 1882 and from August 1894 this was connected to the L&YR Heap Bridge Branch (opened 1874) which linked up with the Bury to Heywood main line. In 1894 Duxbury's purchased Peckett W/No.569 of 1894 to shunt its new sidings. Expansion of the works in 1908 led to the purchase of Peckett W/No.1159 of 1908, while in November 1932 they acquired (second-hand) Peckett W/No.1370 of 1915. June 1944 saw the arrival of Andrew Barclay W/No.945 of 1904. All four locos were 0-4-0 saddle tanks. Barclay 945 is in steam on 17 March 1973, shortly before the works railway finally closed in October 1973. It was one of the very last non-NCB steam operated industrial railways in Lancashire.

The development of fireless locomotives can be traced back to the nineteenth century when early machines were produced in, for example, the USA, Belgium, France and Germany. In the UK the first fireless was not produced until 1912, when Barclay built a loco of this type for a War Office explosives depot. Barclay's went on to specialise in this type and built more than all the other British builders put together. Simply put, the fireless loco's 'boiler' was actually a pressurised reservoir that was charged with water and steam. The driver drew steam out of the reservoir to work the cylinders until a fall in water level – with a gradual fall in tractive effort – required a return to the charging point for a top-up of steam. Because these locos had no live fire, and no exhaust, they were ideal for working at explosives depots, food factories, chemical works, and any site with a ready supply of steam. Andrew Barclay W/No.2268 was delivered to Glaxo Laboratories Ltd of Ulverston (SD 306777) on 7 September 1949, and photographed in action there on 16 May 1977.

The town of Whitehaven stands just north of St Bees Head on the Cumbrian coast. It is a fascinating town, with countless interesting buildings, a harbour and a rich industrial history based principally in coal and the sea. The south end of the town was steeped in the coal industry, with Wellington Colliery perched on the cliff above the harbour, Haig Colliery on the cliff-top at Kells, and Ladysmith Colliery (NX 964161) a little further south. The last-named was sunk to a depth of 1,090 feet in 1900-02, but closed in December 1931. The site was later redeveloped as a Coal Preparation Plant and, in the early 1970s, had an allocation of six steam locomotives (by four different builders) that were in varying states of decrepitude. On a sunny 14 August 1972 giesl-fitted 'Austerity' 0-6-0 saddle tank STANLEY (Hunslet W/No.3302 of 1945, which was new to Manchester Collieries) was hard at work at Ladysmith CPP.

Albright & Wilson Ltd operated its Marchon Chemical Works on a site (NX 966160) at Kells, adjoining Ladysmith Coal Preparation Plant. In 1980 the company utilised three Sentinel diesel hydraulic locomotives (W/Nos.10085 and 10086 of 1961 and 10206 of 1965) for shunting tanker wagons around its site. Wagons went in and out via a branch line that featured an 840 yard self-acting incline of maximum 1 in 5 gradient, controlled by a 250hp stationary engine built by Tinsley's. Operations on the incline were overseen from a brake house erected above the tracks at the top of the grade. At the foot of the incline the industrial branch connected with the BR Barrow to Workington line, just south of Corkickle station. Operations on the incline are viewed on 22 July 1980, with Sentinel W/No.10085 prominent; these activities had ceased by early 1988.

Haig Colliery was located (NX 967176) half a mile south of Whitehaven harbour. It was sunk between August 1914 and March 1918 on the cliff tops at Kells and all its coal was won from seams laying beneath the sea. Continuing into the 1970s, Haig's coal was initially sent along a line that ran south to Ladysmith Coal Preparation Plant. There the coal was washed, before returning to Haig and, on 9 July 1974, giesl-fitted REPULSE (Hunslet W/No.3698 of 1950) is seen operating on the dramatic cliff-top line between the two locations. The wagons were then despatched via a line that ran northwards, before descending an incline into Whitehaven harbour, and onward to the main line. Haig Colliery received substantial investment by the NCB and became the last pit in Cumbria, but heavy losses led to production ceasing in August 1984, and complete closure came in March 1986. Coal shipments from Whitehaven harbour ceased in January 1982.

Almost any industrial railway enthusiast who was active in the 1970s would name the Waterside railway amongst his favourite sites. This fabulous location was in Ayrshire, based in the small town of Dalmellington, where there were NCB offices, locomotive shed, workshops, coal preparation plant and exchange sidings. The area's industrial history is traced back to 1845 and the formation of the Dalmellington Iron Company, which transformed the district's rural tranquillity with the development of coal and ironstone pits, furnaces, slag tips and brick works, all linked by a network of industrial railways. The iron industry eventually faded out, but coal mining continued into NCB days. By the 1970s just Minnivey and Pennyvenie collieries remained, linked to the Waterside Coal Preparation Plant or 'CPP' (NS 443083) by standard gauge lines which were steam-operated to the end. On 29 May 1978 giesl-fitted outside cylinder 0-6-0 side tank No.24 (Andrew Barclay W/No.2335 of 1953) was shunting side-tipping wagons in the rolling Ayrshire countryside.

Barony Colliery (NS 528217) was located midway between Ochiltree and Auchinleck in Ayrshire. The original shafts were sunk by William Baird & Co Ltd in 1906 and completed in 1912. Coal was sent out via a connection which ran north from the colliery to join on to the old Glasgow & South Western Railway at Barony Junction, about two miles to the north-west of Auchinleck Station. In the late 1960s the colliery retained a pair of veteran Neilson 0-4-0STs (of 1885 and 1894 construction) and steam locomotives were utilised into the 1980s, albeit latterly on a stand-by basis. On 10 June 1981 a pair of Andrew Barclay 0-4-0STs, No.8 (left) and No.16 (respectively W/Nos. 2369 of 1955 and 1116 of 1910) were stabled in the yard, and photographed against the backdrop of the pit's impressive A-frame headgears. The rail connection was removed with effect from 25 May 1986 and the colliery closed in 1989.

Bedlay Colliery was situated (NS 720703) at Glenboig, a few miles north of Coatbridge in Lanarkshire. Sunk in 1905 by William Baird & Co Ltd, it was a gassy pit with thin seams, but its coking coal was always wanted by the local iron and steel industries. At nationalisation in 1947 the colliery had three shafts, the NCB subsequently completing (in 1958) a redevelopment of the pit that included construction of a new coal preparation plant. The colliery was a Mecca for steam enthusiasts who, from adjacent roads, could view operations on the NCB's branch line joining the colliery to BR exchange sidings. Inside cylindered 0-6-0 side tank No.9 (Hudswell Clarke W/No.895 of 1909) was shunting the branch on 17 May 1977, against a background of fields and a distant spoil tip. The colliery was steam worked to the end, which came on Friday 11 December 1981.

One of the most remarkable latter-day industrial railway systems in Scotland was operated at Coatbridge in Lanarkshire by R.B. Tennent Ltd. This internal-user railway operated in and around the company's Whifflet Foundry (NS 738643) and the adjoining Meadow Foundry, linking various workshops, foundries and moulding shops. The trackwork included tiny headshunts, turntables, and several diamond crossings. Steam cranes, electrically powered transfer cars, ladle carriers, and flat wagons (used to move castings around the site) were all to be seen, but the main attraction was the steam motive power. Continuing into the 1980s, a fleet of four 4-wheel, vertical boiler, geared tank locomotives were in daily use. Immaculately maintained (and frequently repaired with parts cast in the company's own foundry) the fleet comprised JOHN (Sentinel W/No.9561 of 1953), RANALD (9627 of 1957), ROBIN (9628 of 1957) and DENIS (9631 of 1958). On a sunny 12 June 1981, RANALD was in action, although the railway was subsequently worked by Sentinel diesel locomotives.

Scotland had a fine mix of industrial steam locations. There were the elite 'celebrity' sites (such as Waterside and Polkemmet) which received a steady flow of enthusiastic visitors, while there were also many run of the mill 'workaday' locations where steam locomotives did an efficient – but largely unheralded – daily job of work. Firmly in the latter category was the Imperial Tube Works, Airdrie, of Stewarts & Lloyds Ltd. Over the years this site (NS 752648) was operated by a trio of 0-4-0STs, the last to arrive being Andrew Barclay W/ No.2287 of 1948, which came in 1964 from S&L's Clydesdale Steel and Tube Works, Mossend. On 29 March 1970 Stewarts & Lloyds Ltd (a company formed in January 1903) was taken over by the British Steel Corporation Tubes Division and, shortly after the take-over, on 18 August 1970, the green livery Barclay was photographed hard at work in Airdrie.

Polkemmet Colliery was situated (NS 936639) in the parish of Whitburn in West Lothian. Sinking of the mine by William Dixon & Company commenced early in World War One, but problems due to the hostilities meant that it was not fully operational until mid-1923. Its principal product was high quality coking coal which was mainly used in Lanarkshire steel works. The pit was taken over by the NCB in 1947 and, during the 1950s, benefited from fairly extensive reconstruction, after which it produced an average of over 2,000 tons of coal per day. The coal was sent out via a steeply-graded line from the colliery to exchange sidings up on Polkemmet Moor. From there a mineral branch ran across the moor to Benhar Junction (connection with the ex-CR/LMS Edinburgh-Glasgow line) and to the former NBR/LNER Bathgate-Morningside line (closed 1964). On 1 June 1978 two Barclays (see next caption) set off for the exchange sidings with a rake of loaded wagons.

The line up to Polkemmet exchange sidings was very steep and so, on a daily basis, the coal trains were double-headed. On average eight 300-ton coal trains a day were worked up the bank, and enthusiasts flocked to watch the spectacle. Having battled to the top of the gradient, the loaded coal wagons were left in the sidings for collection by BR, while the colliery engines coupled on to empties which were taken down-grade and left at the screens. After filling with coal, the wagons were marshalled together and collected by the double-header steamers, in a cycle that continued day after day. On 1 June 1978 two Andrew Barclay locomotives (see also previous picture) attack the bank: leading is 0-6-0 saddle tank No.25 (W/No.2358 of 1954) with giesl-fitted 0-6-0 side tank No.8 (W/No.1296 of 1912) coupled behind. Steam working finished in the summer of 1980 and thereafter 350hp class 08 diesel-electric shunters were hired from BR. The underground workings flooded during the 1984/85 strike and the pit never worked again, officially closing in June 1986.

Kinneil Colliery (NS 986812) was on the south bank of the Firth of Forth at Bo'ness in West Lothian. Numerous pits were sunk in the area over the years, and Kinneil was actually a redevelopment (from June 1951) in the yard of Furnaceyard Colliery, in search of high quality coking coal. In April 1964, after eighteen months of digging, Kinneil was linked by a 3½ mile tunnel beneath the Forth to Valleyfield Colliery in Fife, and thereafter most of the two pits' production was raised and processed at Kinneil's preparation plant. On 20 May 1977 the preparation plant yard was being energetically shunted by 0-4-0 saddle tank No.6 (Andrew Barclay W/No.2043 of 1937) which had – surprisingly – an open-back cab. Kinneil Colliery closed in 1982, and No.6 later worked at Bedlay Colliery.

Frances Colliery was situated at Dysart (NT 310939) at the east end of Kirkcaldy in Fife. The pit was sunk on Blair Point by the Earl of Rosslyn's Collieries Ltd and production commenced in 1878, with most of the coal workings beneath the Firth of Forth. It was taken over by the Fife Coal Company in 1923, and the NCB in 1947. Coal was sent out via a standard gauge branch line that ran westwards from the pit, crossing the A955 road en-route, to join the BR line running northwards out of Kirkcaldy. On 20 May 1977 0-4-0 saddle tank No.21 (Andrew Barclay W/No.2292 of 1951) was working the pit sidings. The use of steam locomotives continued at this location into the 1980s, but the pit never resumed production after the infamous 1984/85 miners' strike, and eventually closed.

The small town of Burntisland is located in Fife, on the north bank of the Firth of Forth, and expanded in keeping with the development of its docks which were promoted by the North British Railway. Burtisland coal dock No.1 opened in December 1876 and exported almost 300,000 tons of coal in its first full year of operation. The town was served by the main line Fife coast railway which ran from Inverkeithing, and up to Kirkaldy and points north. The British Aluminium Co Ltd set up a works at the west end of Burntisland, located (NT 225862) alongside, and connected to, this main line. At its works the company utilised a 2ft 0in gauge railway, operated by two Ruston & Hornsby diesels, but the site was best known for its standard gauge system. The BACo was always willing to allow enthusiasts to visit its internal railway, where the three steam locomotives were maintained in pristine mechanical and cosmetic condition. This trio of 0-4-0 saddle tanks were all purchased new for the Burntisland works and comprised Peckett W/Nos.1376 of 1915 and 1579 of 1921, plus Andrew Barclay W/No.2046 of 1937. On 16 August 1972 the eldest Peckett was standing outside the shed, by now out of use, since two John Fowler class 421 diesels had arrived late in 1971 to take over the shunting duties. Peckett W/No.1376 left Burntisland in April 1973, bound for preservation at the Lochty Private Railway, Anstruther, although these days it can be found at the Caledonian Railway, Brechin.

In many ways the decade of the 1970s was both a zenith and a decline of industrial railways. A zenith because the decade saw more industrial railway enthusiasts than ever before, with many who mourned the end of steam on BR finding a new interest in privately-owned systems. A decline because the same decade witnessed the death-throes of industrial steam, plus the scrapping of many early diesel-mechanical shunters and countless items of interesting old rolling stock. At New Stubbin Colliery, Rawmarsh, South Yorkshire (SK 427967) the scrap merchant who purchased the fleet of wooden wagons came up with a novel idea. He set all the wagons on fire and, when the wooden bodies had burned away, it left him with just the scrap metal. The first wagon in the colliery's fleet, number NSb1, is seen in flames on 3 November 1978.

fit food

body + soul
fit food
teresa cutter

low-carb   gluten-free   low-fat   wheat-free

NEW
HOLLAND

First published in Australia in 2004 by
New Holland Publishers (Australia) Pty Ltd
Sydney • Auckland • London • Cape Town

14 Aquatic Drive Frenchs Forest NSW 2086 Australia
218 Lake Road Northcote Auckland New Zealand
86 Edgware Road London W2 2EA United Kingdom
80 McKenzie Street Cape Town 8001 South Africa

National Library of Australia Cataloguing-in-Publication Data:

Cutter, Teresa.

Body + soul : fit food.

Includes index.
ISBN 1 74110 156 5.

1. Cookery. I. Title.

641.5

Publishing Manager: Robynne Millward
Editor: Jenny Scepanovic
Designer: Karlman Roper
Production Manager: Linda Bottari
Printer: Tien Wah Press (Pte) Ltd, Singapore

10 9 8 7 6 5 4 3 2 1

Note:
Cup and spoon measurements in this book
are Australian and therefore metric:
1 cup = 250 ml, 1 tablespoon = 20 ml.

Conversions are approximate. Oven
temperatures are a guide only: always
check your manual.

Acknowledgments

Thank you Paul, my husband and best friend, for all your support and for giving me the courage to believe that dreams can come true. Also for bringing the food to life with your beautiful photography.

Thanks to Fiona Schultz and Robynne Millward from New Holland who saw my vision and made this book possible.

Many thanks also to the News Ltd team from the *Sunday Telegraph* who supported me, including Jeni Cooper and Jody Scott and the fantastic marketing team.

body+soul

body+soul

body+soul

body+soul

body+soul

body+soul

body+soul

body+soul

body+soul

Contents

Introduction

Fit Food contains healthy recipes that are not only good for you but will delight your tastebuds as well. If you love your body and want to stay fit and feel good the best thing you can do is to nourish yourself with foods that will build health and strength. This book focuses on healthy cooking and eating, and uses a variety of natural ingredients including fresh fruits and vegetables, nuts, wholegrains and lean protein sources to feed the body and comfort the soul. Some recipes are vegetarian or vegan but you can easily add animal products to these if you want to.

Low-carbohydrate and low-fat diets are becoming more and more popular due to the quick results in loss of body fat, and many people these days suffer from wheat and gluten allergies or intolerance. So, in this book I've included plenty of low-carbohydrate and low-fat meals and loads of wheat- and gluten-free recipes for breakfast, lunch, dinner and those sweet little indulgences. I've marked each recipe so that you can pick and choose according to your needs:

Gluten-free : Gluten is a protein found in cereals such as wheat, rye, barley, oats, triticale. If you're allergic or intolerant to gluten you're often very restricted as to what you can eat because it's present in so many foods. When you see this symbol, the recipe is free of gluten. (Be aware that malt is contained in many soy milks as it's made from barley, so make sure to purchase malt-free soy milk for recipes in this book. Also make sure you read the labels when purchasing food products for recipes if you're intolerant to gluten.)

Low-carb: If you're on a low-carb eating plan these recipes are for you. These dishes help to change your metabolism so that you burn fat instead of glucose—you'll burn body fat for energy instead of storing it. Theses recipes are also low in fat.

Low-fat: All these recipes are low in fat—approximately 1–10 g of fat per serve—but not at the expense of the tastebuds! They are simple to make, good for you and a healthy addition to your low-fat cooking repertoire.

Wheat-free: If you're wheat intolerant you can still enjoy most of the delicious recipes in *Fit Food*. Be sure to read the labels when purchasing your food products for the recipes to ensure they are wheat-free.

I believe that food should be uncomplicated, quick and simple to make and *Fit Food* is a collection of my best recipes—delicious, balanced meals that will keep you healthy and lean. This book is for everyone interested in light, fresh cooking and a healthy lifestyle. I hope you enjoy some of my favourite recipes.

Healthy eating is easy

Whether you're cooking at home or out for dinner it's easy to get into the habit of choosing healthy food options. In the following sections I give you the best methods for low-fat, healthy cooking, and what to eat when you're out and about.

Low-fat, healthy food should be quick and easy to make. Aim for balanced meals, cook with food that's good for you and control your portions—simple! These habits soon become a way of life and once your eating is on the right track you'll be amazed at how good you feel.

Healthy cooking begins when you're shopping. Think about the meals you're going to make for breakfast, lunch and dinner, as well as snacks, for the coming week. Make a list and stick to it. Base your meals around fresh produce such as vegetables and fruit, and if life is just too hectic for shopping, get onto the web and order your groceries on-line. Stock up on good store cupboard essentials like dried beans and pulses. Canned fish is also a good standby for busy people and easy to toss through al dente pasta or noodles for a quick meal. A few jars of ready-made tomato sauce never go astray, as well as bottles of soy and fish sauce (nam pla) in the fridge to mix with your steamed rice. Toss in a little flaked nori seaweed for extra minerals.

When you're cooking at home, avoid using too much saturated fat. Your food should be simple, fast and fresh so that the food retains most of its nutrients. When cooking, use little or no oil, and use flavoured stock or water instead of oil when frying.

In desserts, cakes and wholegrain breads it's okay to add a little fat in the form of vegetable and nut oils that have no saturated fat and are good for your body. Fruit and vegetable purees such as apple sauce, and mashed bananas and pumpkin are an ideal healthy replacement for fats in dessert and cake recipes. People always ask me, 'How can you cook that without butter and still make it taste good?' Well, all I can say is, you can! You just need to take a different approach to cooking.

Water-soluble vitamins are delicate and easily destroyed during preparation and cooking. Always scrub vegetables rather than peel them, as many nutrients are found close to the skin. If you like to boil vegetables, keep the vitamin-rich water and use as a stock. Include more stir-fry recipes in your diet—stir-fried vegetables are cooked quickly to retain their crunch and nutrients.

Salt is a traditional flavour enhancer, but research suggests that a high-salt diet could contribute to a range of disorders including high blood pressure. Don't automatically salt your food—taste it first. Add fresh herbs or lemon juice close to the end of cooking time or to cooked vegetables—these can enhance flavours in the same way as salt. Choose fresh or frozen vegetables, since canned vegetables tend to be packaged with too much salt.

Steaming

Steamed vegetables are wonderful finished off with a light squeeze of lemon and sprinkled with freshly chopped herbs—enjoy the munching and savour the taste of the fresh flavours. There's no need to coat vegetables with lots of oil or butter. Vegetables can take from 3–10 minutes depending on their type and thickness. Greens like asparagus, bok choy, cabbage and snow peas only take a few minutes, followed by harder vegetables like carrots and cauliflower that take about 8–10 minutes. Other ways of steaming are pan steaming and cooking en papillote. To pan steam, cook veggies in a small amount of stock or water—the liquid reduces while the vegetables cook, so keep adding a little amount of liquid to the pan until cooking has finished and food is tender. When cooking en papillote, top seafood or vegetables with aromatics such as herbs or spices then drizzle with a little stock, soy sauce, water or juice. The food is then wrapped in baking paper or foil and baked in a hot oven—cooked to perfection by the steam from the liquid used.

Poaching

Poaching is a delicious and quick way of cooking without any added fat, and the flavoursome poaching broth can be sipped with the meal or made into a sauce. Poaching works best with delicate pieces of fish or chicken. Done correctly, the food is tender and moist. To poach properly, bring the poaching liquid—fresh spring water, stock or juice—to the boil and reduce to a simmer. The food to be poached must be fully immersed in the liquid and must not be allowed to boil, otherwise delicate protein becomes tough, and fruits turn into purees. This is a very quick process so it's a good idea to keep an eye on the simmering pot. Fish takes about 3–5 minutes depending on the thickness, chicken breasts take about 8 minutes. Reduce the poaching liquid and thicken with a little cornflour to make a delicious, light sauce to accompany the meat.

Stir-frying

Stir-frying can easily be done without the use of any fat whatsoever. Make sure your wok or pan is well heated before you start adding ingredients. Start off with onions and dry cook for 2 minutes. Add ¼ cup of water and watch them caramelise before your eyes. Add other vegetables, meat and flavourings. Fast fit food in five minutes. Not bad!

Grilling

Under or over direct high heat, it doesn't matter. You don't have to add any fat—maybe just a little sea salt and a splash of wine! Delicate fish can be wrapped in banana leaves. Lean meat can be marinated to add flavour—forget the oil marinades and stick to herbs, fruit juices and wines. Chunks of fruit can be brushed with honey and lime then caramelised to perfection. A whole grilled meal can be served with an accompaniment of salsas, mustards and yoghurt. Ten minutes to prepare, five minutes to cook.

Baking, roasting and braising

The wonderful concentrated flavour and aroma of baked and roasted food is just too good to resist. Bake wholegrain breads, cakes and muffins using fruit and vegetable purees and low-fat yoghurt instead of butter. Use less-refined sugars such as honey, juice concentrates and pure maple syrup rather than sugar. Add wheatgerm, dried fruits, nuts and seeds to top it all off. When roasting foods, it's really as simple as moving food directly from the fridge into the oven. Trim all visible fats from meats and cover the base of the pan with water or stock instead of oil. Add fresh herbs and place into a hot oven for the required time. Roast vegetables in large chunks or keep whole. Sprinkle with a little stock, water or fruit juice to keep moist. Braising fresh vegetables and lean meats is my favourite way of cooking. It takes about 1–2 hours but the results are well worth the time spent. Braising is basically casserole-style hot-pot cooking—all ingredients are cooked in the oven or slowly on top of your stove. Think coq au vin, think osso bucco, and you get the picture. Delicious, tender and flavoursome without the use of added fat.

Eating out

People always ask me what they should order when they go out, so I hope this helps with your decision-making next time you're faced with choosing something healthy when you're out to eat.

Buffets are just the worst places for eating too much. For breakfast, avoid fatty meats like sausages and bacon, and ask the chef to poach or boil you a couple of eggs instead of the standard scrambled eggs cooked with lots of butter and cream. Opt for healthier options like fresh fruit, low-fat yoghurt, wholegrains, miso soup and steamed rice. Sorry! No croissants, Danish or brioche please. Yes, they might taste good, but you'll soon be loosening your belt or buying a larger pair of pants. For lunch and dinner, stay clear of the salads tossed with too much mayonnaise and choose fresh, crisp salad leaves instead.

If you're watching your weight or have special dietary needs, when you're going to dine out it's a good idea to get a look at the menu early so you can check out your choices. Give the restaurant a ring and enquire about the cooking methods and if the chef can accommodate your specific requirements. It's best to do this the day before, as it can sometimes be a pain for chefs to have to diverge from the set menu during peak hour service.

Don't starve yourself before going out to restaurants. You'll be much more in control when it comes to ordering and eating.

Ask for sauces and dressings on the side, so that you can choose how much you want or whether you have them at all. Stay clear of hollandaise, bernaise, béchamel, veloutés, aioli, or any cream or butter sauces. These are all major fat closets so opt for a squeeze of lemon or a tomato-based sauce instead.

Water water water! Water is a must at the table. Drink lots of it. It will keep you hydrated, especially if you're drinking wine, and it will keep you full and satisfied so you don't pick at the bread basket in front of you.

When ordering soups, stick to consommés, clear vegetable broths or tomato-based soups. Any creamy soups, chowders and veloutés contain a heap of hidden fat in the form of cream, butter and egg yolks.

When ordering dessert it's a good idea to stick to fruit-based desserts like fresh fruit platters, strudels, sorbets and compotes. Or go halves: if you just can't resist that chocolate cake on the menu, order it and share with someone else.

Bircher muesli

Blueberry and apple muffins

Breakfast pizza

Strawberry energiser

Protein power shake

Hotcakes with berry compote

Oatmeal porridge with apples and walnuts

Soft-boiled eggs with soldiers

Papaya and honeydew melon
with cottage cheese and roasted cashew nuts

Lemon-scented polenta porridge

Vanilla and cinnamon French toast
topped with grilled bananas

Banana and blueberry bread

Pikelets with raspberries and passionfruit

Green fruits in lime and mint

Omelette with wok-tossed vegetables

Wholemeal fruit bread

Fresh berries with roasted almonds

Teresa's recovery breakfast

Wake up to breakfast

If you want a faster metabolic rate, you should always eat a good breakfast. Aim for a balanced, healthy breakfast with a relatively low glycaemic index (GI).

Try to include some protein with your carbohydrate, as it will keep you fuller for longer and keep you more alert throughout the day. Choose calcium-rich protein foods like yoghurt, milk or calcium-fortified soy milk, and blend into a smoothie with a little protein powder and fresh fruit. Other good breakfast proteins are cottage cheese, continental cheese, ricotta, beans, nuts, fish and eggs. Good carbohydrate sources are rice, wholegrain breads, fresh fruits and wholegrains such as oats, barley and buckwheat.

Make sure you read the labels when purchasing food products for recipes if you are intolerant to wheat or gluten.

It doesn't take long to prepare a good, healthy breakfast, even when you're really busy. Just remember that breakfast is the most important meal of the day.

Bircher muesli

Serves 4

1 cup rolled oats
2 cups apple or pear juice
½ cup diced dried apricots or peaches
2 tablespoons pumpkin seeds
2 tablespoons sunflower seeds
2 tablespoons whole almonds, chopped
400 g (13 oz) low-fat natural yoghurt
4 green apples
Juice from 1 pink grapefruit
2 tablespoons pure maple syrup
1 punnet blueberries

In a bowl, combine oats and apple or pear juice.
Let stand in the refrigerator for at least one hour or overnight.

Add dried fruit, seeds and almonds then fold in yoghurt.
Just before serving, grate apples on a mandolin into fine, long strips.
Combine with the grapefruit juice, maple syrup and blueberries.

To serve, spoon muesli into four serving bowls, top with
a sprinkling of grated apple and blueberry salad and mix through.

Variation:
Use any seasonal
fruits, such as
strawberries,
bananas or
mangoes, in
place of the
blueberries.

Low-fat

Wheat-free

Blueberry
and apple muffins

Makes 12

2 cups wholemeal flour
1 teaspoon cinnamon
2 teaspoons baking powder
½ cup raw sugar
3 egg whites
1 cup unsweetened apple sauce
½ cup low-fat milk or soy milk
2 tablespoons macadamia nut oil or light olive oil
¾ cup dried apricots, chopped
250 g (8 oz) blueberries

Preheat oven to 180°C (350°F/Gas Mark 4).

Combine the flour, cinnamon, baking powder and sugar in a bowl
and mix well.
Add the egg whites, apple sauce, milk and oil. Mix until just combined.

Gently fold in dried apricots and blueberries. Spoon into prepared
muffin tins and bake for 25–30 minutes until cooked through and golden.

Note:
Take care not to
overcook the
muffins to ensure
they remain moist.

Variation:
Use spelt flour in
place of the
wholemeal flour if
you're intolerant
to wheat.

Low-fat

Breakfast pizza

Serves 2

6 egg whites
2 whole eggs
Pinch of sea salt and freshly ground black pepper
Olive oil spray for cooking
4 tomatoes, sliced
4 balls bocconcini
2 tablespoons basil, shredded

Beat all the eggs and salt and pepper until combined.

Pour into a hot non-stick pan sprayed with a little olive oil.

Cook like an omelette, over a medium heat until mixture is almost set.

Arrange the tomato slices and bocconcini in layers over the egg.

Place under a hot grill and cook until cheese melts slightly and starts to colour.

Turn out onto two plates and garnish with shredded basil to serve.

Variation:
Replace the bocconcini with low-fat cottage or ricotta cheese. Serve eggs on top of toasted wholegrain or wheat- and gluten-free bread if desired.

Low-carb

Gluten-free

Low-fat

Wheat-free

Strawberry energiser

Serves 1

1 cup low-fat natural yoghurt
Handful of ice
1 punnet strawberries
1 teaspoon honey or maple syrup

Combine all the ingredients and blend until smooth and creamy.

Drink immediately.

Protein power shake

Serves 1–2

1½ cups icy-cold low-fat milk or soy milk
Handful of ice
3 tablespoons vanilla protein powder or skim milk powder
250 g (8 oz) fresh or frozen blueberries

Combine milk, ice, protein powder and berries and blend until smooth.

Drink immediately.

Note:
**There is no need
to use ice if using
frozen blueberries.**

Low-carb

Gluten-free

Low-fat

Wheat-free

Hotcakes with berry compote

Serves 6

Berry compote
300 g (10 oz) raspberries
3 tablespoons honey
¼ cup orange juice
250 g (8 oz) raspberries (extra)
250 g (8 oz) blueberries

Hotcakes
2 cups organic spelt flour
2 teaspoons baking powder
1 teaspoon cinnamon
2 tablespoons honey
½ cup unsweetened apple sauce
¾ cup natural low-fat yoghurt
½ cup low-fat milk or soy milk
3 egg whites, beaten to soft peaks
Olive oil spray for cooking

First make the compote by combining 300 g (10 oz) of the raspberries with the orange juice and honey in a blender. Pour sauce through a strainer and discard the seeds. Add the rest of the berries to the sauce and mix through well.

To make the hotcakes, combine flour, baking powder and cinnamon in a bowl. Add honey, apple sauce, yoghurt and milk then mix through until combined. Gently fold in the beaten egg whites.

Using a heaped tablespoon of batter per hotcake, cook in a non-stick pan sprayed with a little olive oil over a medium heat until golden on both sides.

Stack three hotcakes onto each serving plate and spoon over compote. Enjoy!

Variation:
Plain flour can be used in place of the spelt flour.

Low-fat

Oatmeal porridge
with apples
and walnuts

Serves 2

1 cup water
2 cups low-fat milk or soy milk
1½ cups rolled oats
Pinch of sea salt
1 apple, peeled and sliced
¼ cup walnut halves
¼ cup pure maple syrup or honey

Bring the water and milk to the boil. Add the oats and salt and cook over a low heat stirring constantly for 5–8 minutes until oatmeal is plump and tender. Meanwhile, warm the apple slices with the walnuts and maple syrup.

To serve, spoon the piping hot oats into two serving bowls. Top with the caramelised apple and walnuts.

Note:
This makes a great nourishing and warming breakfast to feed body and soul.

Low-fat

Wheat-free

Vanilla and cinnamon French toast topped with grilled bananas

Serves 4

4 egg whites
½ teaspoon ground cinnamon
2 tablespoons pure maple syrup
2 teaspoons vanilla extract
½ cup low-fat milk or soy milk
8 slices wholegrain fruit bread, toasted
4 firm lady finger bananas
Pure maple syrup or honey to serve

Beat egg whites with the cinnamon, maple syrup, vanilla and milk.

Dip the bread into the egg white mixture and cook over a medium heat in a non-stick pan on both sides until golden.
Meanwhile, slice the bananas and heat for 1 minute under the grill or in a frying pan sprayed with a little olive oil.

To assemble, lay two pieces of the toast onto a serving plate.
Top with sliced bananas and pour over maple syrup or honey to serve.

Low-fat

Papaya and honeydew melon with cottage cheese and roasted cashew nuts

Serves 4

1 honeydew melon
1 small papaya
250 g (8 oz) skim milk cottage cheese or low-fat ricotta cheese
40 g (1½ oz) roasted cashew nuts

Peel the melon and papaya and remove the seeds.
Slice into thick portions and layer alternately onto serving plates.

Top with cheese and cashew nuts. Serve immediately.

Variation:
Use other nuts such as almonds or brazil nuts instead of the cashews.

Low-carb

Gluten-free

Low-fat

Wheat-free

Lemon-scented polenta porridge

Serves 4

3½ cups water
150 g (5 oz) polenta
1 teaspoon salt
2 teaspoons vanilla extract
1 teaspoon coconut essence
Finely grated zest from 1 lemon
Juice from 1 lemon
¼ cup pure maple syrup or honey
½ cup low-fat coconut milk or malt-free soy milk
4 bananas, sliced
1 punnet blueberries
2 tablespoons flaked toasted almonds

Bring water to the boil and pour in polenta. Turn down to a gentle simmer.

Add the salt, vanilla, coconut, lemon zest, juice, maple syrup and coconut milk.

Cook over a gentle heat stirring frequently for about 20–25 minutes until nice and thick.

Divide between serving bowls. Top with sliced banana, blueberries and toasted almonds.

Gluten-free

Low-fat

Wheat-free

Soft-boiled eggs
with soldiers

Serves 2

4 eggs at room temperature
Sea salt and freshly ground black pepper to taste
4 slices wholemeal bread, cut into fingers

Place eggs into a saucepan filled with cold water, covering them by 5 cm.
Cook eggs for 3½ minutes then take out of water immediately. Remove top
of shells and season with salt and pepper.

Serve immediately in egg cups accompanied by freshly toasted fingers of bread.

Note:
Fresh eggs should be brought to room temperature before being boiled.

Variation:
Wrap toast fingers or grissini sticks in smoked salmon before dipping into egg yolk.

Low-fat

Banana and blueberry bread

Makes 1 loaf

1½ cups wholemeal self-raising flour
½ cup wheatgerm
½ cup skim milk powder
1 teaspoon cinnamon
2 large (1 cup) mashed bananas
Grated zest from 1 orange
2 teaspoons vanilla extract
4 egg whites
½ cup pure maple syrup
250 g (8 oz) fresh or frozen blueberries
½ cup dried apricots, chopped

Preheat oven to 180°C (350°F/Gas Mark 4)

In a mixing bowl, combine flour, wheatgerm, skim milk powder and cinnamon.

In a separate bowl, combine mashed bananas with the orange zest, vanilla, egg whites and maple syrup.

Pour mashed banana mixture into the flour and mix through until combined. Fold in blueberries and dried apricots.

Pour into a loaf tin lined with baking paper and bake for about 50 minutes. Cover with foil halfway through cooking to stop over-browning if necessary. Remove bread from the oven and cool before serving topped with sliced banana.

Note:
This is great by itself or topped with sliced bananas and blueberries with a drizzle of honey for breakfast. Also try it toasted the next day spread with low-fat cottage cheese and a drizzle of honey or rice syrup.

Low-fat

Pikelets with raspberries and passionfruit

Serves 4–6

200 g (6½ oz) almond meal
1 cup vanilla protein powder or skim milk powder
1 teaspoon gluten-free baking powder
2 tablespoons low-carb sweetener
1 cup low-fat buttermilk
4 egg whites at room temperature
Olive oil spray for cooking
2 punnets raspberries
Pulp from 6 passionfruit
2 tablespoons pure maple syrup

In a bowl, combine almond meal, protein powder, baking powder and sweetener. Pour in the buttermilk and mix well until combined.

Beat the egg whites until stiff peaks form then fold into the pikelet batter.

Spray a non-stick pan with a little oil spray and heat. Using a heaped tablespoon of batter per pikelet, cook pikelets over a low heat until golden on both sides. Be careful to watch them, as they brown quickly.

Serve alone, or with raspberries and combined passionfruit pulp and maple syrup drizzled on top.

Variation:
Other seasonal fruits can be used to serve with the pikelets.

Low-carb

Gluten-free

Low-fat

Wheat-free

Green fruits in lime and mint

Serves 4

1 honeydew melon, cut into chunks
2 green apples, cut into chunks
4 kiwi fruit, peeled and sliced
2 cups green grapes
2 tablespoons mint, chopped

Dressing
2 tablespoons apple or pear juice concentrate
Juice from 1 lime

In a bowl, combine all the fruits and mint. Pour the dressing over the fruit and mix well.
Serve alone or with low-fat yoghurt, ricotta or cottage cheese.

Dressing Combine concentrate and lime juice in a separate bowl and stir.

Gluten-free

Low-fat

Omelette with wok-tossed vegetables

Serves 1

250 g (8 oz) assorted mushrooms
1 clove garlic
¼ cup red capsicum, finely chopped
¼ cup yellow capsicum, finely chopped
1 teaspoon wheat-free tamari soy sauce
Freshly ground black pepper
1 whole egg
3 egg whites
Sea salt and freshly ground black pepper to taste
1 tablespoon water
Olive oil spray for cooking
1 tablespoon chives, chopped
Bean shoots (optional)
Spring onions, sliced (optional)

Sauté the mushrooms and garlic in a wok with a little water until golden.
Make sure to use only a little water at a time, otherwise the mushrooms will
stew instead of frying. Add the capsicum, tamari and black pepper.
Toss through well and keep warm.

Beat the eggs thoroughly with the salt, pepper and water. Heat a frying pan
until very hot then lightly spray with a little olive oil. Pour in the eggs. Shake the
pan and stir with a fork at the same time, moving the curds from the edge of
the pan to the centre as it sets.

When the curds are just firm but still soft, leave over the heat for a few seconds
to set the base. Take off the heat. Spoon in the mushroom and capsicum filling
and sprinkle with chives.

Use a fork to release the omelette from opposite sides of the pan and fold into
the middle. Turn out onto a warm serving plate and serve immediately, garnished
with bean shoots and spring onions.

Low-carb

Gluten-free

Low-fat

Wheat-free

Wholemeal fruit bread

Makes 2 loaves

625 g (20 oz) wholemeal flour
1 teaspoon cinnamon
½ teaspoon ground ginger powder
1 teaspoon salt
16 g (½ oz) dried yeast
50 ml (2 fl oz) honey
370 ml (12 fl oz) warm water
2 tablespoons macadamia nut oil or light olive oil
700 g (23 oz) dried fruits, chopped (apricots, pears, dates, figs, sultanas)
1 egg, lightly beaten
2 tablespoons low-fat milk or soy milk

Combine the flour, spices, salt and yeast and mix well. In a separate bowl, combine the honey, water and oil, then pour into the flour. Mix well until you form a nice dough. Knead well for about 10 minutes until the dough is smooth and elastic.

Form the dough into a ball and with a knife score a large cross in the middle of the dough. Place in a large bowl and cover with plastic wrap. Leave in a warm place for 1–1½ hours until it has doubled in size.

Turn out onto a work surface and knead in the dried fruit until all mixed through. Shape into two free form loaves.

Place onto a baking tray lined with baking paper or dusted with flour and leave in a warm place for 1 hour to rise.

Preheat oven to 200°C (400°F/Gas Mark 6).

Brush the loaves with combined egg and milk using a pastry brush.

Bake the loaves for 18–20 minutes then turn down the heat to 180°C (350°F/Gas Mark 4) and finish baking the loaves for a further 18–20 minutes. Cover with foil if necessary to prevent over-browning. Cool before slicing to serve.

Note:
This is a lovely, moist fruit bread that is delicious fresh or toasted for breakfast. Serve alone or topped with cottage cheese or tahini, or sliced banana and honey.

Variation:
Add 180 g (6 oz) chopped walnuts to the recipe if desired.

Low-fat

Fresh berries
with roasted almonds

Serves 4

2 punnet strawberries, washed and halved
1 punnet blueberries
1 punnet raspberries
1 tablespoon apple juice concentrate (optional)
4 tablespoons roasted almond flakes
Low-fat ricotta, yoghurt or cottage cheese

Combine berries in a bowl and pour over the apple juice concentrate
to sweeten slightly. Place into a serving bowl and sprinkle with
roasted almond flakes.

Serve with low-fat yoghurt, or ricotta or cottage cheese on the side.

Low-carb

Gluten-free

Low-fat

Wheat-free

Teresa's recovery breakfast

Serves 1–2

2 slices rye bread
2 heaped teaspoons sugar-free blueberry jam
4 tablespoons cottage cheese or low-fat ricotta
100 g (3½ oz) fresh blueberries
30 g (1 oz) almonds, chopped

Toast the rye bread and spread with the jam then cottage cheese.

Top with the blueberries and almonds. Eat and enjoy!

Note:
I like to have this for breakfast or as a morning snack after a workout in the gym.

Variation:
Try adding a teaspoon of crunchy peanut butter onto the rye bread before you add the jam.

Low-fat

Butterfly pasta salad

Asparagus frittata

Sushi pockets

Swordfish salad with lime and chilli dressing

Chunky bean minestrone

Lentil and carrot soup

Potato and salmon cakes

Wholesome brown rice salad

Chicken noodle soup

Chicken coleslaw with coconut lime dressing

Wholemeal spaghetti with tuna, olives, lemon and garlic

Salad leaves with beef and seaweed lime dressing

Wholemeal pita stuffed with smoked salmon salad

Tuna tabouli

Chilli squid

Noodle salad

Mango and chicken san choy bau

Energise with lunch

Even if you've had a power breakfast, it's important that you also have a good, healthy lunch. You're still active at this time of day, so the food you eat will be burned off and will help you make it through the rest of the afternoon. If you skip lunch, you often end up craving fats and sugar by four o'clock, so you start dipping into the biscuits and tend to overeat in the evening.

Lunch should be a combination of lean protein, wholegrains and vegetables. Try including a variety of vegetables such as green beans, mushrooms, capsicum, cauliflower, cabbage and crisp leafy salad greens. Cooked dried beans and pulses, chicken and turkey breast, lean beef, eggs, tinned fish, cottage cheese, pasta and noodles are also great low-GI foods that will keep you going until dinner.

Butterfly pasta salad

Serves 2

1 cup shelled broad beans
1 cup peas
4 bunches asparagus, tips only
2 cups freshly cooked butterfly (farfalle) pasta
2 teaspoons olive oil or flax seed oil
2 tablespoons lemon juice
150 g (5 oz) red cherry tomatoes, halved
150 g (5 oz) mini yellow tomatoes, halved
2 tablespoons parsley, freshly chopped
2 tablespoons basil, freshly chopped
Sea salt and freshly ground black pepper to taste
4 tablespoons low-fat ricotta
2 tablespoons grated parmesan (optional)

Blanch broad beans, peas and asparagus in boiling water for 1 minute then drain.
Combine in a bowl with pasta, olive oil, lemon juice, tomatoes, herbs and seasoning.
Toss well.

Divide between serving plates and top with a dollop of low-fat ricotta and sprinkle with parmesan if desired.
Serve immediately.

Note:
This salad is also delicious with tinned or smoked salmon or tuna added to the recipe.

Low-fat

Asparagus frittata

Serves 1

1 bunch asparagus, cut into 5-cm lengths
4 egg whites
1 whole egg
1 teaspoon grated lemon zest
1 tablespoon parsley, freshly chopped
Sea salt and freshly ground black pepper to taste
Olive oil spray for cooking
2 tablespoons low-fat ricotta or cottage cheese
1 tablespoon low-fat grated tasty cheese

Cook the asparagus in boiling water for 1 minute then drain.

Beat the egg whites, lemon zest, parsley, salt and pepper in a bowl.

Heat a non-stick frying pan over a moderate heat and spray with a little olive oil spray.
Pour in the egg mixture then top with the asparagus and ricotta or cottage cheese.
Cover and cook until the eggs have set on the bottom.

Sprinkle the top with grated cheese and finish off under a grill or in a hot oven until the top
is set and golden.
Serve warm.

Variation:
Top frittata with chunky tomato salsa, smoked salmon or grilled prawns.

Low-carb

Gluten-free

Low-fat

Wheat-free

Sushi pockets

Serves 2–4

2 cups brown rice, cooked and cooled
2 cloves garlic, crushed
4 shiitake mushrooms, chopped
1 bunch spinach, finely shredded
¼ cup roasted cashew nuts
2 spring onions, sliced
1 cucumber, finely diced
1 red capsicum, finely diced
½ cup coriander, finely chopped
1 packet prepared tofu bags (yamato ajitsuke inari)

Dressing

¼ cup mirin
2 tablespoons wheat-free tamari soy sauce
1 tablespoon tahini (sesame seed paste)

Combine rice, garlic, mushrooms, spinach, nuts, spring onion, cucumber, capsicum and coriander into a bowl. Pour over dressing and mix through the rice and vegetables. Stuff into prepared tofu bags and serve.

Dressing Combine mirin, soy and tahini in a small bowl and mix well.

Note:
These can be made well in advance of serving. Salad can be eaten without being stuffed in the bags. Add beans to the mixture for extra protein.

Gluten-free

Low-fat

Wheat-free

Swordfish salad
with lime and chilli dressing

Serves 4

2 large handfuls mixed salad leaves
2 large handfuls bean sprouts
2 spring onions, sliced
1 red, yellow and orange capsicum, sliced
1 bunch coriander, chopped
1 bunch mint leaves
½ juicy pineapple, peeled and cut into chunks
Sea salt and freshly ground black pepper
4 x 200 g (6½ oz) swordfish steaks
1 teaspoon olive oil

Dressing
2 cloves garlic, crushed
1 stick lemon grass, finely chopped
½ cup lime juice
1 tablespoon honey
1 red chilli, chopped
2 tablespoons fish sauce (nam pla)

First prepare the salad ingredients by combining the salad leaves, bean sprouts, spring onion, capsicum, coriander, mint and pineapple chunks. Season with salt and pepper. Divide between 4 serving bowls.

Heat the oil on a hot grill plate and cook the swordfish for about 2–3 minutes each side until cooked through. Remove from the hot plate.

Break up each piece of swordfish into large chunks and place on top of the individual salads. Pour over a little dressing and serve.

Dressing Crush the garlic and lemon grass in a mortar and pestle. Add the rest of the dressing ingredients and combine well.

Note:
Substitute the fish with cold, poached chicken breast or tinned tuna in spring water if desired.

Low-carb

Gluten-free

Low-fat

Wheat-free

Chunky bean minestrone

Serves 4–6

1 onion, diced
2 cloves garlic, chopped
3 sticks celery, finely chopped
2 large carrots, diced
1 red capsicum, diced
1 yellow capsicum, diced
1 x 400 g (13 oz) tin crushed tomatoes
2 x 400 g (13 oz) tins mixed beans
½ cup green peas
4 cups gluten-free vegetable stock
2 tablespoons chopped parsley
Sea salt and freshly ground black pepper to taste

In a large pot, sauté the onion and garlic in a little water until soft.
Add the celery, carrot and capsicum and cook for a few minutes.

Add the crushed tomatoes, mixed beans, peas and stock.
Simmer over a gentle heat for 15 minutes until vegetables are tender.

Season with salt and pepper and fold through chopped parsley just before serving.
Serve hot.

Low-carb

Gluten-free

Low-fat

Wheat-free

Lentil and carrot soup

Serves 6–8

375 g (¾ lb) red lentils
6 cups gluten-free vegetable stock
3 large organic carrots, grated
1 teaspoon cumin
1 teaspoon ground turmeric (optional)
1 teaspoon ground coriander (optional)
Sea salt and freshly ground black pepper to taste

Yoghurt cream

300 ml (10 fl oz) natural yoghurt
1 tablespoon lemon juice
2 tablespoons coriander, chopped
2 tablespoons mint, chopped
½ cucumber, seeded and finely chopped

Combine lentils and stock in a large saucepan and bring to the boil.
Add carrots and spices, cover and simmer over a gentle heat for 15 minutes
until lentils are tender. Add more stock if necessary.

Take off the heat and cool then blend or process until smooth. Season with salt
and pepper. To serve, spoon soup into bowls and top with yoghurt cream.

Yoghurt cream Combine all ingredients in a bowl and mix well.

Low-carb

Gluten-free

Low-fat

Wheat-free

Potato and salmon cakes

Makes 4 patties

1½ cups cold mashed potatoes
1 x 200 g (6½ oz) tin pink salmon, drained
½ cup cooked green peas
2 spring onions, chopped
¼ cup parsley, chopped
½ cup fresh wholemeal breadcrumbs or almond meal
Sea salt and freshly ground black pepper to taste
2 beaten eggwhites for coating
1 cup wholemeal breadcrumbs for coating
Grated zest from 1 lemon
Olive oil spray for cooking

Combine potatoes, pink salmon, peas, parsley, spring onions and breadcrumbs and mix well. Season to taste with salt and pepper.

Form mixture into 4 patties and dip each patty into the beaten egg, then roll in combined breadcrumbs or almond meal and lemon zest.

Spray a non-stick pan with a little olive oil spray and heat. Cook cakes for a few minutes each side until warmed through and golden. Serve with salad leaves.

Note:
Patties can be baked in a hot oven for 15–20 minutes, instead of fried.

Variation:
For a wheat- and gluten-free version, substitute almond meal for the breadcrumbs. Tuna can be used instead of salmon.

Low-fat

Wholesome
brown rice salad

Serves 4

4 cups cooked brown rice
2 cloves garlic, crushed
1½ cups or 400 g (13 oz) tin cooked brown lentils, drained
3 spring onions, chopped
1 bunch chives, chopped
750 g (1½ lb) roasted pumpkin, cut into chunks

Dressing

1 tablespoon white miso paste
1 tablespoon tahini (sesame seed paste)
¼ cup lime juice
1 tablespoon pure maple syrup
Sea salt and freshly ground black pepper to taste

In a large bowl combine brown rice, garlic, lentils, spring onions, chives and pumpkin.

Pour dressing over salad and toss well.

Spoon into serving bowls and enjoy!

Dressing Combine all ingredients in a small bowl and stir well.

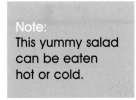

Note:
This yummy salad
can be eaten
hot or cold.

Gluten-free

Low-fat

Wheat-free

Chicken noodle soup

Serves 4

8 cups chicken stock
2 cloves garlic, chopped
1 tablespoon grated ginger
2 sticks lemon grass, finely chopped
2 whole skinless chicken breasts
250 g (8 oz) shiitaki mushrooms
2 heads broccoli cut into flowerets
1 x 250 g (8 oz) packet dried soba noodles

Combine chicken stock, garlic, ginger and lemon grass in a large saucepan and bring to the boil. Add the chicken breasts and gently simmer for 8–10 minutes until cooked through.

Add the mushrooms and broccoli and simmer for a further 3–5 minutes.

Meanwhile, cook noodles in plenty of boiling water until al dente then drain. Divide between serving bowls.

Remove chicken breast from the soup and slice the meat. Return the sliced chicken meat back to the soup and stir through.

Ladle the soup over the noodles and serve immediately.

Variation:
For a gluten-free version, use rice noodles and gluten-free stock.

Low-carb

Low-fat

Chicken coleslaw
with coconut lime dressing

Serves 2

1 large carrot, finely grated
¼ cabbage, finely sliced
1 red capsicum, thinly sliced
1 yellow capsicum, thinly sliced
2 spring onions, sliced
2 cloves garlic, crushed
1 bunch mint, chopped
1 bunch coriander, chopped
Freshly ground black pepper to taste
1 chicken breast, cut into strips
2 tablespoons natural, low-fat yoghurt
2 tablespoons sesame seeds to coat
Sea salt to taste
1 teaspoon olive oil

Dressing
½ cup low-fat coconut milk
2 tablespoons fish sauce (nam pla)
1 teaspoon honey
¼ cup lime juice

Place carrot, cabbage, capsicum, spring onion, garlic and herbs into a salad bowl, season with black pepper and toss.

Coat the chicken in the yoghurt and sesame seeds, season with a little salt and lightly sauté in the oil until cooked through.

Pour the dressing over the salad and mix well. Season to taste.

Divide between serving bowls and top with chicken. Serve immediately.

Dressing Combine all ingredients in a small bowl and stir well.

Low-carb

Gluten-free

Low-fat

Wheat-free

Wholemeal spaghetti with tuna, olives, lemon and garlic

Serves 2

200 g (6½ oz) wholemeal spaghetti
2 cloves garlic, finely chopped
1 x 185 g (6 oz) tin tuna in spring water
8 black olives
Juice from ½ lemon
1 tablespoon parsley, chopped
1 teaspoon olive oil
Freshly ground black pepper to taste
1 tablespoon parmesan cheese, freshly grated (optional)

Cook pasta in plenty of salted, boiling water until al dente. Drain well and pour into a large serving bowl.

Add the garlic, tuna, olives, lemon juice, parsley, oil, pepper and parmesan cheese if using.

Toss well and serve immediately.

Variation:
For a gluten-free version, use rice noodles or gluten-free pasta.

Low-fat

Salad leaves with beef and seaweed lime dressing

Serves 2

2 x 150 g (5 oz) pieces lean steak
1 teaspoon olive oil
Sea salt
Assorted salad leaves, enough for 2 people
¼ avocado, thinly sliced

Dressing
Juice from 2 limes
¼ cup mirin
1 teaspoon sesame oil
1 tablespoon nori seaweed, finely shredded

Rub the steaks with the olive oil and sea salt and cook in a hot non-stick pan until cooked to medium. Take off the heat and allow to rest.

Meanwhile, combine salad leaves into serving bowls.
Slice the beef and place on top of the salad then arrange avocado on top.
Pour dressing over the salad and serve.

Dressing Combine all ingredients in a small bowl and mix well.

Variation:
Garnish with marigold leaves for a pretty effect.

Low-carb

Gluten-free

Low-fat

Wheat-free

Wholemeal pita stuffed
with smoked salmon salad

Serves 1

1 wholemeal pita bread, cut in half
Handful lettuce leaves
Few sprigs of mint and coriander
100 g (3½ oz) smoked salmon
½ cucumber, sliced into ribbons with a vegetable peeler
1 bunch asparagus, trimmed
½ yellow capsicum, sliced
¼ red onion, sliced

Open the cavity of the pita bread and fill with the salad ingredients.
Alternatively leave the pita bread whole. place the salad in the middle and roll up.

Variation:
Use a gluten-free rice or corn flat bread in place of the pita.

Low-fat

Tuna tabouli

Serves 2

1 cup continental parsley, chopped
½ cup mint, chopped
250 g (8 oz) red cherry tomatoes, halved
4 shallots, chopped
2 cloves garlic, chopped
¼ cup raw almonds, chopped
¼ cup pumpkin seeds
¼ cup sunflower seeds
1 x 185 g (6 oz) tin tuna in spring water
Light pinch of ground cumin
Juice from 1 lemon
1 tablespoon olive oil
Sea salt and freshly ground black pepper to taste

In a salad bowl, combine the parsley, mint, tomatoes, shallots, garlic, almonds and seeds then mix through. Add the tuna, cumin, lemon juice, olive oil and mix through well. Season with salt and pepper.

Note:
This makes a scrumptious and simple, light lunch that will satisfy any palate.

Low-carb

Gluten-free

Low-fat

Wheat-free

Chilli squid

Serves 2

3 tubes cleaned squid, cut into portions and scored
1 red chilli, sliced
3 cloves garlic, chopped
1 teaspoon sesame oil
2 tablespoons wheat-free tamari soy sauce
4–5 tablespoons mirin
Baby spinach leaves to serve

Combine squid with chilli, garlic, sesame oil, tamari and mirin. Marinate for 30 minutes then cook in a hot non-stick pan for a couple of minutes until tender.

Serve on top of spinach leaves.

Variation:
Use other seafood such as prawns, firm white fish, scallops or lobster in place of the squid.

Low-carb

Gluten-free

Low-fat

Wheat-free

Noodle salad

Serves 2–3

¼ cup dried hijiki seaweed

200 g (6½ oz) green tea soba noodles or any other noodle

1 cup shelled green soy beans or any other bean

Dressing

4 tablespoons wheat-free tamari soy sauce

4 tablespoons mirin

1 teaspoon sesame oil

1 clove garlic, crushed

Reconstitute the seaweed by soaking in cold water for 30 minutes, then drain.

Boil the noodles in plenty of water until al dente then drain and rinse under cold running water.

Place into a large bowl along with the seaweed and shelled soy beans.

Pour dressing over the noodles, toss well and serve.

Dressing Combine all ingredients in a small bowl and stir well.

Variation:
Wakaeme seaweed can be used in place of the hijiki. Other pulses and beans like chickpeas, white beans or broad beans can be used in place of the soy beans. Use rice noodles for a gluten-free version.

Low-fat

Mango and chicken san choy bau

Serves 2

2 chicken breasts, poached and shredded
1 ripe mango, peeled and finely diced
1 red capsicum, diced
½ cup coriander, chopped
1 cucumber, diced
¼ cup lime juice
3 tablespoons gluten-free sweet chilli sauce
1 small lettuce

Combine all the ingredients, except for the lettuce, in a bowl.

Wash the lettuce well and separate the leaves into cups.

Spoon filling into the lettuce cups and serve.

Variation:
Use seafood such as prawns or firm white fish in place of the chicken.

Low-carb

Gluten-free

Low-fat

Wheat-free

Whole baked snapper

Fish and chunky chips

Bigos with veal schnitzel

Veal marsala with rocket and parmesan

Warm prawn salad

Soy- and mirin-glazed lamb with sweet potato mash

Beef fillet with carrot and daikon radish fettuccini

Swordfish kebabs

Low-carb bolognaise

Grilled chicken breast with vegetable fettucine

Stir-fried chicken with mushrooms and cashew nuts

Warm fish pie

Fish with sweet soy sauce on spinach

Poached chicken with wok-tossed snow peas

Spaghetti carbonara

Chilli crab

Seafood hot pot

Nourish with dinner

Our metabolic rate slows down in the late afternoon and evening, so unless you're very active, it makes good sense to eat most of your food spread throughout the day—not one huge meal at night as so many of us do.

Remember to keep portions controlled and don't overload your dinner plate unless it's with lots of leafy salad and vegetables. Eating lots of antioxidant-rich vegetables will nourish your immune system and keep you looking lean and healthy.

When cooking with meat, make sure you use nice lean cuts and trim off any visible fat before you cook it. Get a good non-stick frying pan and sauté all your food in minimal oil, or in a little water or stock instead. When frying, adding small amounts of water throughout the cooking process to cut the fat and keep the moisture in the food.

Whole baked snapper

Serves 2–3

1 whole small snapper
1 lemon, sliced
Sea salt and freshly ground black pepper to taste
2 bunches bok choy, washed and quartered
2 cloves garlic, crushed
1 teaspoon sesame oil
2 tablespoons wheat-free tamari soy sauce
¼ cup mirin

Preheat oven to 220°C (425°F/Gas Mark 7).

Make three slashes on each side of the cleaned fish and fill the cavities with
slices of lemon. Season fish with salt and pepper. Place onto a baking tray lined
with baking paper and bake for 15–20 minutes until cooked through.

While fish is cooking, sauté the bok choy with the garlic and sesame oil until just wilted.
Add the tamari and mirin and toss through.

To serve, arrange snapper onto a serving plate then place bok choy at the side.
Drizzle the pan juices over the fish and serve.

Low-carb

Gluten-free

Low-fat

Wheat-free

Fish and chunky chips

Serves 4

8 large potatoes, washed and cut into chunky wedges
Olive oil spray for cooking
Sea salt and freshly ground black pepper to taste
4 x 180 g (6 oz) tuna steaks
2 tablespoons sesame seeds

Preheat oven to 220°C (425°F/Gas Mark 7).

Boil the potatoes for 5 minutes in salted water then drain well and place in a bowl.

Spread out potatoes on a baking tray lined with baking paper and spray with a little olive oil then season with salt and pepper. Bake in the oven for 25–30 minutes until golden and cooked through.

Meanwhile, season the tuna steaks with salt and pepper and sprinkle one side with the sesame seeds. In a hot non-stick pan, sear on one side until golden, turn over and cook over a medium heat for a further 2 minutes until just cooked through.
Serve immediately with the chunky chips.

> **Note:**
> **Serve this meal with a crunchy green salad and a low-fat mayo, or chunky tomato salsa for a low-carb version.**

Gluten-free

Low-fat

Wheat-free

Bigos with veal schnitzel

Serves 4

Bigos

½ savoy cabbage, finely shredded
2 onions, finely diced
4 cloves garlic, finely chopped
1 cup chicken stock
150 g (5 oz) lean bacon, chopped (optional)
2 carrots, peeled and grated
2 x 440 g (14 oz) tins sauerkraut, well drained
2 bay leaves
Sea salt and freshly ground black pepper to taste

Veal schnitzel

4 x 120 g (4 oz) veal steaks
Sea salt and freshly ground black pepper to taste
Flour to dust
3 beaten egg whites
2 cups fresh wholemeal breadcrumbs to coat
Olive oil spray for cooking

To make the bigos, boil a large pot of water, remove from heat and add the cabbage. Leave for 10 minutes and drain well. Place into a large, deep baking dish.

Sauté onion and garlic in a non-stick pan with a little stock until softened and golden. Add the bacon if using and cook with a little stock until browned. Remove and add to the cabbage along with the grated carrots.

Place the sauerkraut into a colander and rinse well in cold water. Drain well and add to the baking dish along with the rest of the ingredients. Add bay leaves and season with salt and pepper. Mix ingredients until well combined. Cover with foil and bake for 45 minutes–1 hour.

To make the schnitzel, preheat oven to 200°C (400°F/Gas Mark 6).

Flatten out veal until it's nice and thin. Season and dust with flour, dip into the egg whites then the breadcrumbs to coat.

Place veal onto a baking tray lined with lightly oiled baking paper. Spray a little olive oil over the top and bake in oven for 10 minutes on each side until golden. Serve hot on top of the bigos.

Note:
Bigos is a delicious and healthy baked cabbage dish from Poland. This is my grandmother's recipe. It can be eaten by itself or with the schnitzel. If making without the schnitzel, add 500 g (16 oz) diced chicken breast with the onion and garlic.

Variation:
This dish is lovely served with a Napolitano sauce over the top of the veal.

Low-carb

Low-fat

Veal marsala
with rocket and parmesan

Serves 2

4 x 120 g (4 oz) veal steaks
4 lean slices prosciutto
12 sage leaves
1 teaspoon olive oil
Freshly ground black pepper
1 clove garlic, chopped
½ cup marsala
2 large handfuls rocket leaves
½ cup shaved parmesan cheese

Press a slice of prosciutto onto each piece of veal and top with three sage leaves.

Heat the olive oil in a non-stick pan over a medium to high heat and cook the veal, sage leaves down, for one minute until golden. Season with black pepper then turn over and cook the other side for one minute.

Pour over the marsala and simmer for a few seconds until slightly thickened.

Place veal onto serving plates with combined rocket and parmesan salad. Drizzle the sauce over the veal. Serve immediately.

Low-carb

Gluten-free

Low-fat

Wheat-free

Warm prawn salad

Serves 2

4 oranges, segmented
1 large handful bean shoots
1 handful bean sprouts
2 cups sweet papaya, chopped
½ cup coriander, chopped
¼ cup mint, chopped
½ red onion, sliced
2 spring onions, sliced
½ yellow capsicum, sliced
1 teaspoon sesame oil
12 uncooked prawns, peeled with tails intact
Sea salt to taste
Sprinkle of roasted peanuts or cashew nuts to garnish (optional)

Dressing
Juice from 4 oranges
¼ cup lime juice
1 tablespoon honey
2 tablespoons fish sauce (nam pla)
2 cloves garlic, chopped
1 red chilli, chopped

In a serving bowl, combine oranges, bean shoots, sprouts, papaya, coriander, mint, red onion, spring onion and capsicum.

Heat sesame oil in a hot non-stick pan and sauté the prawns for a minute until just cooked and golden. Season with a little sea salt.

Pour the dressing over the salad and toss well. Arrange into serving bowls. Top with prawns and garnish with a few peanuts or cashews.

Dressing Combine all ingredients in a small bowl and stir well.

Variation:
Sweet pineapple can be used in place of the papaya.

Low-carb

Gluten-free

Low-fat

Wheat-free

Soy- and mirin-glazed lamb with sweet potato mash

Serves 4

800 g (1½ lb) sweet potato, peeled and chopped into chunks
¼ cup low-fat coconut milk
½–1 teaspoon fresh ginger, grated
¼ teaspoon ground cinnamon
Sea salt and freshly ground black pepper to taste
2 lean lamb backstraps
1 teaspoon sesame oil
1 tablespoon wheat-free tamari soy sauce
4 tablespoons mirin
4 tablespoons water

Steam or boil the sweet potato until tender then drain well. Mash with the coconut milk, ginger and cinnamon until lovely and smooth. Season to taste with sea salt and pepper.

Rub the lamb with the sesame oil and cook in a hot non-stick pan until golden and still a little pink in the centre.

While the lamb is still in the pan, add combined soy, mirin and water and simmer until it forms a syrupy sauce. Remove from heat.

To serve, dollop mash onto serving plates. Slice the lamb diagonally and arrange on top of the mash. Pour over the sauce and serve immediately.

Note:
Serve this dish with a large garden salad.

Gluten-free

Low-fat

Wheat-free

Beef fillet with carrot and daikon radish fettuccini

Serves 2

2 large carrots
1 large daikon radish
2 x 180 g (6 oz) beef fillets
1 teaspoon sesame oil
6 shiitake mushrooms
1 tablespoon miso paste
¼ cup mirin
¼ cup water
1 teaspoon olive oil
1 tablespoon toasted sesame seeds
Sea salt and freshly ground black pepper to taste
Bean sprouts and spring onions, sliced, to garnish

Peel carrots and radish. Run carrots and daikon radish along a mandolin to form nice, long fettucine strips. Place in a bowl of cold water and set aside.

Rub the beef fillets with the sesame oil and sear in a hot non-stick pan on one side for 3–4 minutes until browned. Turn over and cook on the other side until steaks are done to your liking.

Add the mushrooms then combined miso paste, mirin and water. Cook until sauce thickens slightly. Remove from heat.

While beef fillet is cooking, drop the vegetable fettuccini into a pot of lightly salted boiling water and cook for 3 minutes until just tender, but still holding its shape. Drain well and toss gently with olive oil and sesame seeds. Season to taste.

To serve, divide vegetable fettuccini between two serving dishes and top with beef fillets, followed by a little sauce and mushrooms. Garnish with sprouts and spring onions and serve immediately.

Low-carb

Gluten-free

Low-fat

Wheat-free

Swordfish kebabs

Serves 2

350 g (11½ oz) swordfish steaks, cut into cubes
½ red capsicum, cut into chunks
½ yellow capsicum, cut into chunks
2 tablespoons teriyaki sauce
2 tablespoons water
1 cup hot cooked brown rice
4 large bunches spinach, blanched and chopped
2 tablespoons roasted cashew nuts, chopped
Sea salt to taste

Thread the fish and capsicum onto skewers. Cook in a hot non-stick pan until fish
is cooked and golden.

Combine teriyaki sauce and water then pour over the kebabs in the pan to coat.

Meanwhile, combine the hot rice with the spinach and nuts. Divide between two serving
bowls and top with the kebabs. Serve immediately.

Low-fat

Low-carb bolognaise

Serves 4

1 onion, diced
2 cloves garlic, chopped
500 g (16 oz) lean topside, minced
1 large carrot, grated
1 stalk celery, finely diced
2 tablespoons tomato paste
2 cups beef stock
800 g (1½ lb) ripe tomatoes, peeled, seeded and chopped,
   or 2 x 425 g (13½ oz) tins crushed tomatoes
6 green zucchini
6 yellow zucchini
1 teaspoon olive oil
¼ cup parsley, chopped
2 teaspoons raw sugar
Sea salt and freshly ground black pepper to taste
2 tablespoons freshly grated parmesan (optional)

Sauté the onion and garlic in a little water until softened. Add the beef and cook, stirring constantly for 5 minutes, until browned. Add the carrot and celery and cook for a further 5 minutes, adding a little water if necessary.

Stir through the tomato paste, stock and tomatoes. Cover and cook over a low heat for 45–60 minutes until the sauce is thick and rich.

While sauce is cooking, run the zucchini along a mandolin to form nice, long spaghetti strips. Just before serving, blanch zucchini in salted boiling water for 1 minute to heat through, then drain. Toss with a little olive oil and a tablespoon of the parsley. Keep warm.

Season sauce to taste with sugar and salt and pepper. Fold in the rest of the chopped parsley just before serving.

Divide zucchini spaghetti into serving bowls and top with bolognaise sauce and freshly grated parmesan if using. Serve immediately.

Low-carb

Gluten-free

Low-fat

Wheat-free

Grilled chicken breast
with vegetable fettucine

Serves 4

4 organic skinless chicken breasts
Olive oil spray for cooking
Sea salt and freshly ground black pepper to taste
3 carrots
3 zucchini
2 cloves crushed garlic
1 onion, sliced
½ red chilli, finely chopped
1 teaspoon olive oil
¼ cup gluten-free chicken stock
1 leek, cut into strips
1 red capsicum, sliced
2 spring onion, sliced
2 tablespoons coriander, chopped

Spray chicken breast with olive oil spray, season and barbecue or pan-fry
until cooked through. Keep warm.

To make the vegetable fettucine, slice the carrots and zucchini into nice, long fettucine strips
on a mandolin and blanch in salted, boiling water for 1–2 minutes until soft, adding the carrots
first then the zucchini for the last minute. Drain well.

Sauté garlic, onion and chilli in olive oil until soft. Add some of the stock followed by the
leek and capsicum then cook for a further few minutes until soft.

Add the spring onion and coriander and season to taste. Add vegetable fettucine and
combine gently.

To serve, divide the vegetable fettucine onto serving plates and top with grilled chicken.

Low-carb

Gluten-free

Low-fat

Wheat-free

Stir-fried chicken
with mushrooms and cashew nuts

Serves 2

2 lean chicken breasts, sliced
2 cloves garlic, chopped
1 red onion, sliced
500 g (16 oz) assorted mushrooms
2–3 tablespoons gluten-free oyster sauce
¼ cup water
2 tablespoons roasted cashew nuts
2 tablespoons coriander, chopped

In a hot non-stick pan, sauté the chicken, onion and garlic until golden. Add the mushrooms followed by the oyster sauce and water and toss until mushrooms have heated through and are slightly golden. Add the cashew nuts and coriander then spoon into serving bowls and serve immediately.

Variation:
Use wheat-free tamari soy sauce in place of the oyster sauce but replace the water with mirin.

Low-carb

Gluten-free

Low-fat

Wheat-free

Warm fish pie

Serves 6

750 g (1½ lb) white fish fillets
Gluten-free chicken stock for poaching
1 leek, chopped
1 onion, chopped
½ cauliflower, chopped and steamed until soft
1 cup low-fat coconut milk
½–1 cup stock from poaching liquid
Sea salt and freshly ground black pepper to taste
2 cups green peas
¼ cup freshly chopped coriander
750 g (1½ lb) pumpkin, peeled and chopped
6 slices low-fat cheese

Place fish into a saucepan and pour over enough chicken stock to cover. Slowly bring to the boil and gently simmer for about 8 minutes until cooked through. Remove from the stock and cool.

Sauté leek and onion in a little water until soft. Combine with the cauliflower, coconut milk and a little of the poaching liquid into a food processor and blend until smooth, thick and creamy. Add more poaching liquid if necessary. Season with salt and pepper. Pour cauliflower mix into a bowl.

Cut the fish into small pieces and add to the cauliflower sauce along with the peas and coriander. Mix through well. Divide into individual ovenproof dishes.

Cook pumpkin until tender and mash. Season with salt and pepper. Spoon over the fish pies and top with a slice of cheese. Bake in a moderate oven 180°C for 25 minutes until heated through and serve immediately.

Variation:
You can use potatoes in place of the pumpkin in this recipe.

Low-carb

Gluten-free

Low-fat

Wheat-free

Fish with sweet soy sauce
on spinach

Serves 2

2 x 185 g (6 oz) fish fillets
1 teaspoon sesame oil
2 tablespoons sweet soy sauce
½ cup chicken stock
4 bunches spinach leaves
2 cloves garlic
1 tablespoon soy sauce
½ cup chicken stock

Sear each side of the fish in a hot pan with sesame oil for 2–3 minutes until just done, adding
a little stock if necessary during the cooking. Add sweet soy sauce and rest of the stock and
heat through until fish has been glazed by the sauce.

Meanwhile, stir-fry the spinach with the garlic, soy and stock until wilted. Place into serving bowls
and top with the fish.

Low-carb

Low-fat

Poached chicken
with wok-tossed snow peas

Serves 4

4 cups gluten-free chicken stock for poaching
4 organic chicken breasts
1 red chilli, sliced
1 teaspoon sesame oil
2 cloves garlic, finely chopped
4 large handfuls of snow peas
3 tablespoons wheat-free tamari soy sauce
6 tablespoons mirin
½ cup chopped fresh coriander and parsley combined
Grated zest from 2 lemons

Bring the chicken stock to a low simmer. Add the chicken and gently poach for about 8–10 minutes until cooked through. Turn off the heat, leaving the chicken in the stock while you do the snow peas.

In a hot pan, sauté the chilli and garlic in the sesame oil for a few seconds then add the snow peas, tamari and mirin. Toss well for a minute until heated through but still crisp.

To assemble, divide the snow peas between serving plates. Slice each chicken breast into 3–4 pieces and sprinkle with combined herbs and lemon zest. Arrange over the snow peas and serve immediately.

Low-carb

Gluten-free

Low-fat

Wheat-free

Spaghetti carbonara

Serves 2

250 g (8 oz) spaghetti
30 g (1 oz) finely shaved prosciutto, sliced
2 cloves garlic, chopped
150 g (5 oz) finely shaved ham, left whole
½ cup evaporated skim milk
30 g (1 oz) parmesan cheese, finely grated
2 tablespoons parsley, chopped
Freshly ground black pepper

Place the spaghetti in boiling salted water and cook until al dente.

Meanwhile, in a frying pan cook proscuitto, garlic and ham until crisp and golden.

Add the skim milk along with the spaghetti, parmesan and parsley and heat through.
Add more milk if necessary. Season with pepper and divide between serving plates
to enjoy with a nice, crisp salad.

Variation:
For a gluten-free
version use
gluten-free ham
and pasta.

Low-fat

Chilli crab

Serves 2

4 blue swimmer crabs, cleaned and halved
1–2 red chillies, chopped
1 teaspoon sesame oil
4 cloves garlic, chopped
Juice from 2 limes
3 shredded kaffir lime leaves
¼–½ cup water or stock
4 tablespoons wheat-free tamari soy sauce
¼ cup mirin
1 red capsicum, sliced
¼ cup coriander, chopped

Place the crabs in a hot, deep pan with the chillies, sesame oil, garlic, lime juice, lime leaves and water or stock. Cover and cook for 10–15 minutes stirring occasionally until crab has cooked through. Add a little more water or stock to the pan if necessary to help with the cooking. Remove the lid then add the tamari, mirin and red capsicum. Cook for a few minutes until sauce has thickened then fold through the coriander.

Serve with salad leaves and fresh limes.

Low-carb

Gluten-free

Low-fat

Wheat-free

Seafood hot pot

Serves 4

2 onions, sliced
2 cloves garlic, chopped
2 tablespoons laksa paste
3 cups chicken stock
1 cup light coconut milk
1 x 225 g (7 oz) tin bamboo shoots
600 g (20 oz) white fish fillets, cut into cubes
500 g (16 oz) mussels, cleaned
250 g (8 oz) prawn meat
1 bunch choy sum or spinach leaves
1 red capsicum, diced
¼ cup coriander, chopped

Sauté onion and garlic with a little water until soft. Add laksa paste followed by the stock and coconut milk. Bring to the boil and turn down to a simmer. Add the bamboo shoots, seafood, choy sum and capsicum. Cover and simmer for 10 minutes until seafood has cooked and choy sum has wilted. Add more stock if necessary. Fold through coriander just before serving.

Ladle into bowls and serve hot with freshly steamed seasonal vegetables and a squeeze of lemon over the top.

Low-carb

Low-fat

Coconut banana crème brûlée

Mini meringues

Strawberry baskets

Mango passionfruit pavlovas

Angel food cake

Sweet melon and lime martini

Berry yoghurt ice-cream

Berry sauce

Chocolate brownies

Warm fig and apple strudel

Chunky chocolate chip cookies

Tiramisu

Wholemeal carrot cake

Raspberry, apricot and coconut cake

Lemon and blueberry polenta cake

Lamingtons

Strawberry shortcakes

Sweet and delicious

We all love to bite into lovely moist cakes and heavenly desserts to savour the sweetness and texture. I like making cakes and experimenting with different flours and flavours in my kitchen, developing recipes that most of us can indulge in every now and then. The products of my baking often end up being devoured by our next-door neighbours or the people at the gym where I train.

When making healthy cakes, just a little unsaturated oil will give your cakes a texture and crumb that will win awards. Apple sauce is a good substitute for most of the fat in a cake recipe and it helps create a lovely, moist texture.

Flour is then carefully incorporated with as little stirring as possible. to prevent overworking the gluten, which can produce a tough cake rather than a moist, crumbly masterpiece. I also like using almond meal (ground almonds) as a replacement for flour in many of my low-carb and wheat- and gluten-free recipes. The meal gives a good, crumbly texture and moisture to cakes.

There are many new low-carb and low-GI sweeteners now available in supermarkets, pharmacies and health food stores that don't have the aftertaste of many low-joule sweeteners.

Coconut banana crème brûlée

Serves 2

1 large banana, chopped and frozen
Pulp from 4 passionfruit
300 g (10 oz) firm silken tofu
2–3 heaped tablespoons coconut milk powder or skim milk powder
2 teaspoons coconut essence
2 teaspoons vanilla extract
1 tablespoon honey
2 tablespoons caster sugar or palm sugar to sprinkle

In a food processor, blend all ingredients, except sugar, until smooth.

Divide mixture between two heatproof dishes. Sprinkle the tops with the sugar and grill on high for 1 minute until sugar has caramelised (alternatively a kitchen blowtorch is just great for this job).
Serve immediately.

Note:
This recipe is best made just before serving.

Variation:
Place mixed berries in the bottom of each dish before pouring the mixture in.

Gluten-free

Low-fat

Wheat-free

Mini meringues

Makes 16

2 egg whites at room temperature
100 g (3½ oz) caster sugar
120 g (4 oz) dark chocolate melts
120 g (4 oz) walnuts, chopped

Preheat the oven to 110°C (200°F/Gas Mark ¼).

Beat the egg whites in a bowl until soft peaks form. Gradually sprinkle in the sugar a little at a time, beating well after each addition. Beat well until meringue is smooth and glossy.

Spoon into a piping bag and pipe rounds onto a baking tray lined with baking paper. Bake for about 1¼ hours then cool on the tray.

Melt chocolate in a microwave or in a bowl over a pot of simmering water. Dip the bases of the meringues into the chocolate and then into the chopped nuts. Place back onto the baking tray and allow to cool.

Note:
These are great little treats to serve at dinner parties with coffee.

Low-fat

Wheat-free

Strawberry baskets

Serves 4–6

60 ml (2 fl oz) macadamia nut oil or olive oil
2 teaspoons honey
4 tablespoons icing sugar
6 tablespoons plain flour
2 egg whites
300 g (10 oz) strawberries, washed and halved
1 tablespoon apple juice concentrate

Preheat oven to 180°C (350°F/Gas Mark 4)

Gently heat the oil and honey in a saucepan. Add the icing sugar and cool slightly. Add the flour and egg white and combine well.

Place a tablespoon of mixture onto a sheet of baking paper and spread out into a circle (a good way to do this is to place another piece of baking paper over the top and press down and out gently with your hands, then peel off the paper)

Bake baskets individually in oven for 8 minutes until just golden. Remove immediately with a spatula and shape over the top of a cup or glass to form a cup. Cool.

Combine strawberries and apple juice concentrate and spoon into the baskets. Serve immediately.

Note:
The baskets can be made ahead of time and stored in an air-tight container.

Variation:
Serve the baskets with low-fat ice cream or sorbet for an indulgent treat.

Low-fat

Mango passionfruit pavlovas

Makes 8 individual pavlovas

4 egg whites at room temperature
Pinch of sea salt
¾ cup caster sugar
½ teaspoon lemon juice
2 teaspoons gluten-free cornflour
250 g (8 oz) low-fat smooth ricotta
400 g (13 oz) thick, low-fat vanilla yoghurt
2 mangoes, sliced
Pulp from 6 passionfruit

Preheat oven to 120°C (250°F/Gas Mark ½).

Beat the egg whites with the pinch of salt until frothy and just starting to hold their shape. Slowly add the sugar a little bit at a time, beating well after each addition. Continue to beat well until the whites are smooth and glossy. Add the lemon juice and cornflour and mix through well.

Pipe the meringue onto a large tray lined with baking paper into eight rounds or rings. Bake in oven for 1½ hours then cool in the oven with the oven door slightly open.

To decorate, arrange pavlovas onto serving plates and top with combined ricotta and yoghurt. Arrange mango slices on top and finish with passionfruit pulp. Serve immediately.

Variation:
Use low-fat smooth ricotta cheese in place of the yoghurt.

Gluten-free

Low-fat

Wheat-free

Angel food cake

Serves 10–12

12 large egg whites
2 tablespoons lemon juice
1 heaped teaspoon cream of tartar
½ teaspoon salt
1 cup caster sugar
2 teaspoons vanilla extract
Grated zest from 1 lemon
¾ cup plain flour
1 teaspoon baking powder
½ cup desiccated coconut

Frosting

4 egg whites
¾ cup caster sugar
2 teaspoons vanilla extract

Preheat oven to 180°C (350°F/Gas Mark 4).

In a large mixing bowl, whisk egg whites and lemon juice until light and frothy. Add cream of tartar and salt. Continue beating until whites form soft peaks, but do not over-beat. Slowly sprinkle in sugar a little at a time and beat well until you have a stiff meringue.

Fold in vanilla and lemon zest then flour, coconut and baking powder. Spoon into a prepared 20-cm (10-inch) round cake tin and bake for 35 minutes until the sponge springs back when touched.

Remove sponge from the oven and invert onto a wire rack. Cool completely upside down in the tin. Release gently, running a thin bladed knife around the tin. Generously cover cake with frosting then garnish with rose petals before serving.

Frosting Combine egg whites, sugar and vanilla in a large metal bowl and set over a pot of simmering water. Beat with a handheld electric mixer until thick and creamy.

Variation:
Serve wedges of cake with fresh strawberries or a berry compote.

Low-fat

Sweet melon
and lime martini

Serves 2

Crushed ice to serve
½ honeydew melon cut into small chunks
30 ml (1 fl oz) melon liqueur
Juice from 1 lime
60 ml (2 fl oz) frozen vodka
Soda water

Add the melon chunks to two large martini glasses half-filled with crushed ice.

Pour over melon liqueur followed by the lime, vodka and soda water.

Serve immediately.

Note:
This makes a delicious light dessert and cooling cocktail in one. Make sure you use gluten-free liqueur.

Gluten-free

Low-fat

Wheat-free

Berry yoghurt ice-cream

Serves 8

1 kg natural yoghurt
½ cup honey
2 punnets strawberries, washed and halved
2 punnets raspberries
Finely grated zest and juice from 1 lemon

Combine the yoghurt and honey. In a food processor, blend the berries together until smooth, then add to the yoghurt mixture along with the lemon zest.

Pour into an ice-cream maker along with the lemon juice and churn for about 15–20 minutes or according to the manufacturer's instructions. Store covered in the freezer until needed. Soften ice-cream slightly before serving.

Serve scoops in bowls with berry sauce and extra berries.

Berry sauce

300 g (10 oz) raspberries
1 tablespoon honey
¼ cup orange juice
250 g (8 oz) strawberries, halved
250 g (8 oz) blueberries

Blend together raspberries, honey and orange juice.
Pour through a strainer and discard the seeds.
Mix with the strawberries and blueberries and spoon over the ice-cream.

Gluten-free

Low-fat

Wheat-free

Chocolate brownies

Makes 12–16 pieces

1 cup wholemeal flour
½ cup almond meal
½ cup cocoa powder
1 teaspoon baking powder
Pinch of salt
2 teaspoons vanilla extract
¼ teaspoon almond essence
½ cup macadamia nut oil or olive oil
¾ cup pure maple syrup
2 egg whites
¼ cup low-fat milk or soy milk
½ cup walnuts, chopped
½ cup chocolate, chopped into small pieces

Preheat oven to 180°C (350°F/Gas Mark 4).

Combine flour, almond meal, cocoa, baking powder and salt.

Add vanilla extract, almond essence, oil, maple syrup, egg whites, low-fat or soy milk, walnuts and chocolate. Mix well and spread into a lined square cake tin. Bake in oven for 20 minutes until top is cooked through but still slightly moist in the centre.

Cool in the tin and refrigerate before cutting into squares.

Low-fat

Warm fig and apple strudel

Serves 6

4 large golden delicious apples, peeled and roughly grated
10 dried figs, chopped
½ teaspoon cinnamon
1 tablespoon raw sugar
Grated zest from 1 lemon
Juice from ½ lemon
6 sheets filo pastry
¼ cup oat bran
2 tablespoons almond meal
1 egg white
½ cup macadami nuts (optional)

Preheat oven to 180°C (350°F/Gas Mark 4).

Combine apples, figs, cinnamon, sugar, lemon zest and juice.
On a working surface, lay three sheets of filo pastry in two separate piles and
sprinkle over combined oat bran and almond meal.

Halve apple mixture and place on the pastry sheet piles, forming a log shape
on each with the mixture. Roll up pastry, tucking the ends underneath.

Brush strudels with beaten egg white and top with macadamia nuts if desired. Bake for 25–30
minutes until golden. Cover with foil halfway through the cooking process to prevent
burning if necessary.

Serve with warm low-fat custard.

Low-fat

Chunky chocolate chip cookies

Makes 16 cookies

4 egg whites
½ cup low-carb sweetener
250 g (8 oz) almond meal
½ cup malted milk powder
1 teaspoon baking powder
2 teaspoons vanilla extract
pinch of sea salt
200 g (6½ oz) low-carb dark chocolate squares, chopped

Preheat oven to 180°C (350°F/Gas Mark 4).

Beat egg whites until light and fluffy. Add the sweetener and beat well.

Fold through almond meal, milk powder, baking powder, vanilla, salt and chocolate.

Form into walnut sized balls and place onto a baking tray lined with baking paper.

Bake for 20–25 minutes until golden. Remove from the oven and allow to cool.

Variation:
Caster sugar can be used instead of sweetener in this recipe.

Low-carb

Gluten-free

Tiramisu

Serves 6

650 g (21 oz) low-fat smooth ricotta cheese
2 teaspoons vanilla extract
2 tablespoons pure maple syrup
2 x 200 g (6½ oz) vanilla natural yoghurt
2 tablespoons coffee liqueur
1 tablespoon coffee essence
2 teaspoons good quality cocoa powder
1 cup freshly made plunger coffee
¼ cup pure maple syrup
¼ cup coffee liqueur (extra)
1 small chocolate sponge cake
Cocoa powder for dusting

Beat the ricotta with the vanilla and maple syrup until light, smooth and creamy. Add the yoghurt and liqueur and coffee essence and then mix through.

Divide mixture in half. Mix the cocoa powder into half of the ricotta mixture.

Mix the freshly made coffee with the maple syrup until syrup is dissolved. Add coffee liqueur and cool.

To assemble, break sponge into small, bite-size pieces and place at the base of six serving glasses. Drizzle over a little of the coffee syrup, then spoon a little white ricotta cream over the sponge. Add another layer of sponge followed by a little syrup and then top with the chocolate cream layer.

Continue assembling the layers alternating each colour until you reach the top of the glasses. Refrigerate until serving. Dust with cocoa powder just before serving.

Variation:
Use thin slices of store bought almond bread to garnish if desired. Fresh berries added in between the layers also works well.

Low-fat

Wholemeal carrot cake

Serves 16

½ cup tahini
1 cup pure maple syrup
4 egg whites
300 g (10 oz) silken tofu
2 teaspoons vanilla extract
Grated zest from 1 orange
2 cups finely grated carrot
2½ cups wholemeal flour
2 teaspoons cinnamon
1 teaspoon sea salt
2 teaspoons baking powder
1 cup sultanas
1 cup walnuts, roughly chopped
1 cup unsweetened pineapple pieces, drained

Preheat oven to 180°C (350°F/Gas Mark 4).

Combine tahini, maple syrup and egg whites. Beat well until smooth.

Add the tofu, vanilla and orange zest. Beat well until smooth.

Add the grated carrot and stir through.

Add the flour, cinnamon, salt, baking powder, sultanas, walnuts and pineapple.
Mix through until combined.

Pour into an oiled and lined baking tin. Bake for 1–1½ hours.

Test with a skewer before removing from oven. Cool before serving.

Variation:
Use spelt flour instead of wholemeal flour if you are intolerant to wheat. To make a delicious tofu cream to serve with this cake, whip together 300g (10 oz) firm silken tofu with juice and rind of ½ lemon, 2 tablespoons pure maple syrup and 3 tablespoons coconut milk powder.

Low-fat

Raspberry, apricot and coconut cake

Serves 16

300 g (10 oz) almond meal
1½ cups low-carb sweetener
1½ cups skim milk powder
1½ cups desiccated coconut
12 egg whites
Juice from 1 orange
Grated zest from 2 oranges
2 teaspoons coconut essence
200 g (6½ oz) dried apricots, finely chopped
250 g (8 oz) raspberries

Preheat oven to 180°C (350°F/Gas Mark 4).

Combine almonds, sweetener, powder and coconut into a mixing bowl.

Beat the egg whites they form soft peaks then fold through the orange juice and zest, coconut essence, apricots and raspberries.

Pour into a lightly oiled, large square baking tin or lamington tin and bake for 45–50 minutes.

Cool to room temperature before removing from the tin.

Variation:
Caster sugar can be used instead of sweetener in this recipe.

Low-carb

Gluten-free

Low-fat

Wheat-free

Lemon and blueberry polenta cake

Serves 10

2 bananas, mashed
¾ cup pure maple syrup
¼ cup macadamia nut oil or light olive oil
¼ teaspoon sea salt
2 teaspoons vanilla extract
1 teaspoon ground cinnamon
½ teaspoon ground nutmeg
½ teaspoon ground ginger
Grated zest and juice from 2 lemons
½ cup malt-free soy milk
¾ cup polenta
2 teaspoons baking powder
¾ cup pure maize cornflour
¾ cup brown rice flour
1 cup almond meal
½ cup desiccated coconut
250 g (8 oz) blueberries

Preheat oven to 180°C (350°F/Gas Mark 4).

Combine bananas, maple syrup, oil, salt, vanilla, cinnamon, nutmeg and ginger. Mix well until combined. Mix through the lemon juice and zest, milk, polenta, baking powder, flours, almond meal and coconut; batter should be smooth and sticky. Stir in a little more soy milk if not. Add the blueberries and mix through lightly.

Spoon into an oiled baking tin dusted with polenta. Bake for 1 hour until cooked through. Test with a skewer before removing from oven. Cool before serving.

Gluten-free

Low-fat

Wheat-free

Lamingtons

Makes 30

12 egg whites
300 g (10 oz) caster sugar
2 teaspoons vanilla extract
3 teaspoon coconut essence
Grated zest from 1 lemon
1 tablespoon lemon juice
160 g (5½ oz) plain flour
30 g (1 oz) cornflour
Desiccated coconut to coat

Frosting
250 g (8 oz) icing sugar
¼ cup cocoa powder
¼ cup hot skim milk or water

Preheat oven to 180°C (350°F/Gas Mark 4).

Beat the egg whites until fluffy, then slowly add the sugar and beat well until smooth. Add the vanilla, coconut essence and lemon zest and juice, then sift in the combined flours and lightly fold through.

Spoon into a lamington tin lined with baking paper and bake for 30–35 minutes until cooked through. Allow to cool in the tin before turning out onto a wire rack.

Cut the sponge into small squares and dip into frosting, coating well, then roll in the coconut. Place onto a plate and allow to set.

Frosting Sift the icing sugar and cocoa powder into a mixing bowl. Pour in the hot milk or water a little at a time until you have a smooth, runny paste.

Note:
The cake is best made the day before icing.

Low-fat

Strawberry shortcakes

Makes 10

225 g (7 oz) almond meal
¾ cup skim milk powder or low-carb protein powder
¾ cup desiccated coconut
½ cup rice flour
2 teaspoons baking powder
1 cup low-fat milk or malt-free soy milk
Sugar-free strawberry jam to serve
Low-fat smooth ricotta to serve
Fresh strawberries to serve

Preheat oven to 180°C (350°F/Gas Mark 4).

In a bowl, combine the almond meal, milk powder, coconut, rice flour and baking powder. Pour in the milk and mix until combined. The mixture should be slightly wet and sticky.

Flour a board with rice flour and pat out the dough. Cut into rounds and place on to a sheet of baking paper. Bake for 20–25 minutes until golden. Remove from the oven and cool.

Cut shortcakes in half and spread with strawberry jam and ricotta then top with plump, fresh strawberries.

Note:
These cakes are best eaten on the day you make them.

Variation:
Try these for breakfast spread with a little organic tahini and drizzled with raw, natural honey.

Low-carb

Gluten-free

Low-fat

Wheat-free

Glossary

Apple juice concentrate Juice extracted from organic apples and evaporated to form a syrup. Use in place of sugar in cakes, fruit salads and dressings.

Coconut milk Made from blended coconut flesh and warm water strained through a muslin cloth. Available from supermarkets and Asian grocers.

Coriander A herb of which the roots and stems can be used in sauces and stocks, while the leaves can be folded through dishes and used as a garnish. Do not use dry coriander as a substitute as the flavour is not the same. Available in the herb section in supermarkets and Asian grocers.

Fish sauce (nam pla) Prepared from fermented anchovies and salt. Use sparingly in Asian-style dishes; despite its name it doesn't impart a fishy flavour. Available from supermarkets and Asian grocers.

Malt-free soy milk Use malt-free soy milk in recipes if you are intolerant to gluten. A delicious alternative to milk that can be used in cakes, muffins and breads. Use also in low-fat rice puddings and smoothies. Available in supermarkets, health food stores and Asian grocers.

Mirin A natural, sweet rice flavouring used in dressings, sauces and marinades. Used extensively in Japanese cuisine.

Miso A rich paste made from fermented soy beans. The two common types are light (white) miso or dark (red) miso. Use as a flavour base for miso soup, but can be added to most soups, stews, sauces and dressings in place of stock or just to enhance the flavour and nutritional value of a dish.

Oyster sauce Made from oysters, soy and salt. It is available from supermarkets and Asian grocers and has a delicious flavour. Use in marinades, stir-fries or as a sauce base for meats and seafood.

Sea salt Higher in minerals than ordinary table salt and produced by the evaporation of unpolluted sea water. It has a lovely flavour and less is needed than table salt to flavour food.

Sea vegetables Most common varieties are hijiki, kombu, wakame and nori; all rich in essential minerals. Toss seaweed through noodles, salads and steamed rice and add to enhance the flavour and nutritional value of soups, stocks and stir-fries. Available from many supermarkets and Asian grocers.

Soy beans These beans have a delicious buttery taste and can be tossed into salads, stews, stir-fries and soups. They can be found fresh, frozen, canned and dried in supermarkets, Asian grocers or health food stores.

Spelt flour A wholegrain food high in protein, iron and B vitamins. Can usually be tolerated by people who are wheat intolerant, even though the grain is derived from wheat. It is not, however, gluten-free. Available from health food stores.

Tahini A paste made from either raw or roasted sesame seeds. Use in place of butter to spread on bread. It also adds a delicious flavour to dips, sauces and dressings, and can be added to pastry as a binding agent instead of butter.

Tamari soy sauce A rich, dark soy sauce made without wheat. Once opened, the flavour weakens and colour darkens, so it is best to buy it in quantities that you will use quickly. It can be stored at room temperature or refrigerated and is available from supermarkets, Asian grocers and health food stores.

Tofu Made from coagulated soy milk that has been shaped into blocks. It has a neutral taste that marries well with other foods, taking on their flavour. It is available fresh or deep-fried. Store fresh tofu covered in water in the refrigerator and change the water once a day. Use thick and thin deep-fried tofu in soup, stir-fries, salads and curries. Thin tofu can also be filled with sushi rice and eaten cold. When using deep-fried tofu, blanch it first in boiling water to remove excess oil. Store covered in plastic in the refrigerator.

Wholegrains Use organically grown wholegrains high in complex carbohydrates and low in fat such as wheat, rye, oats, millet, rice buckwheat and corn.

Index

About Teresa Cutter

Teresa Cutter is a qualified chef who specialises in creating healthy recipes that taste fantastic and are good for you. She writes a weekly healthy food column and has developed recipes for mainstream weight loss centres around Australia.

   Physical fitness plays a big part in Teresa's life—she is a certified personal fitness trainer and is skilled in martial arts, including full contact Muay Thai kickboxing and ju jitsu wrestling.

   Teresa believes that it's important to have a healthy, balanced diet to enjoy good quality of life and *Fit Food* is a reflection of her passion for fitness and well-being, and healthy cooking.